LEGISLATIVE
LAW AND PROCESS
IN A NUTSHELL

By
JACK DAVIES
Professor, William Mitchell College of Law
State Senator, Minnesota

ST. PAUL, MINN.
WEST PUBLISHING CO.
1975

Davies Leg.Law
2nd Reprint—1976

PREFACE

No attempt is made in this book to draw a distinction between political science and law, for legislation reaches deeply into both fields. Most political scientists and law professors who write on legislation stay on their own ground and consequently fail to discuss facets of the subject from the other discipline, facets which are vital to an understanding of legislation. Students of both law and political science are left misinformed and misled.

Lawyers have not been trained to look at legislation as a dynamic system affecting every aspect of their work. Rather, their training has focused narrowly on legislation as two kinds of documents —statutes already enacted to be read and applied, and bills to be drafted for enactment. The political action by which a bill becomes a statute is thought of as being beyond the concern of lawyers. Political scientists view legislation primarily as a process, and they describe that process as a power struggle. They omit from their studies any explanation of the challenging legal work required to draft a bill and to fit enacted statutes into the world of legal rules already in existence.

This is one book in the nutshell series for law students. It will be valuable in courses on legal process, introduction to law and legislation. But since it extends the story of legislation beyond the legalistic outlook of the usual law school course, the book will be useful to political scientists, to legislators, to legislative staff and to others interested in the complicated institutions that are the legislatures of America.

The book presents legislation as one long, significant, and intellectual journey. It draws attention to the relationship between the means and the ends of that journey. Legislation starts before the legislature is involved; when there exists only hope or anger or disappointment or concern in someone's mind. The book describes what is needed to turn these emotions into ideas and then into solid and responsive legislative bills. It describes the process used to test and refine ideas in legislative institutions. It examines the tactics of advocates which speed, impede, or redirect legislative action. The dynamic life of legislative law after enactment is described, including how agencies, local governments and businesses use statutes and how citizens, lawyers and courts adjust them to fit life's realities.

The basic emphasis is on the story of the power of ideas in the legislative process. This tale is seldom told, yet it provides the most accurate and practical look into the field of legislation. After all is said and done, ideas dominate legislative life.

PROFESSOR JACK DAVIES

St. Paul, Minnesota
June, 1975

This book is dedicated to the south Minneapolis voters who since 1958 have made the legislature a subject of more than academic interest to me.

Senator Jack Davies

*

OUTLINE

OUTLINE

Chapter 3. Advocacy in the Legislature

PART II: MAKING A BILL

Chapter 4. Ideas for Legislation

OUTLINE

XIII

PART III: PERSPECTIVES ON LEGIS-LATIVE POWER

Chapter 6. Legislative Policy Making

Chapter 7. Governing by Legislatures

OUTLINE

Chapter 8. Limitations on Legislative Power

OUTLINE

OUTLINE

PART IV: LEGISLATURES AND COURTS

Chapter 10. Constitutional Tests of Legislation

Chapter 11. Technicalities Affecting Substance

OUTLINE

Chapter 12. Judicial Supervision of Legislative Procedure

†

LEGISLATIVE LAW and PROCESS IN A NUTSHELL

PART I

THE LEGISLATIVE PROCESS

CHAPTER 1

TWO INTRODUCTORY PROPOSITIONS

A. OBLIGATION TO PETITION

§ 1–1. **Board of review.** The single most important duty of legislators is to vote *yes* or *no* on proposed legislation, thereby passing judgment on petitions from those individuals and groups who ask for legislative action. When petitions for legislation are imaginative and sensible, legislators produce good legislation. When proposals are weak and ill-conceived, legislative performance reflects those qualities. Legislatures work almost exclusively as boards of review to judge proposals brought forward by various groups. Legislatures respond, they seldom lead. Those who want something from a legislature must ask for it.

§ 1–2. The silver platter. Legislators are aware in a general way of most problems and ready to make reasonable responses. What they need is detailed advice on how to respond; they need a request for specific legislation. The effective petition is served on a silver platter as a soundly conceived and well-drafted bill. It is accompanied by supporting advocacy which convinces legislators that the bill is sound and that they will not incur serious political vulnerabilities if they support it.

Legislators themselves seldom invent an idea, draft that idea into a bill, educate the press and public to a bill's merits, or lead a lobbying effort in both houses of the legislature and with the executive branch. It is unrealistic to expect them to. What actually happens is that new ideas in the form of bill drafts come to legislators from citizens, scholars, lawyers, bureaucrats, and lobbyists; these non-legislators then help pass the bill by explaining its merits to legislators and to the public. A bill coming from outside the legislature has a political legitimacy—a credential—that the few bills legislators think up on their own do not possess.

§ 1–3. **Malapportioned lobbying.** Lobbyists— persons employed as legislative advocates—do not represent fairly the spectrum of groups affected by legislative action. Many interests lack lobbyists. Legislators try to fill the void with their own examination of each bill presented, but the sheer number of bills undermines this effort. Legislators are generalists who lack specialized knowledge that would aid their review of bills. The pace of most legislative sessions allows them to do little more than judge the cases presented by advocates of competing interests. In the same way that lawyers are necessary to aid judges in appellate and trial courts and to assist officials in administrative proceedings, the informed advocacy of lobbyists is essential to legislators. The legislative process is an adversary system in which silence is treated as acquiescence. If those affected do not object to a bill, legislators tend to accept assertions about its merit from its supporters. It is unrealistic to expect that popularly-elected, modestly-compensated, part-time legislators can, without great assistance, provide public policy leadership for a state.

B. LEGISLATION IS WORDS

§ 2–1. A bill for an act. The formal procedural work of a legislature begins with a set
of words called "A bill for an act."

Under all parliamentary procedure, debate is
out of order until a motion is made. The purpose of requiring a motion is to give focus to the
discussion. In a legislative institution, this practical principle is carried forward by the requirement that a written bill be the object of consideration. Because deliberations are centered on bill
drafts, those interested in a legislative issue know
who is affected and how they are affected. The
words in the bill tell what is involved. Throughout the process the focus is on words; words
which communicate the underlying values, judgments, and purposes of the bill.

A legislature decides whether the words should
be enacted and thus be accorded the legal force
of official legislative action. Public policies adopted by a legislature must be expressed in the words
of an act. Once an act is passed, the legislature's job is done. It is then up to other forces
in society—governmental, commercial, community—to implement the policy, to put the legislative
words to work in real life. The legislature cannot
change that policy without enacting new words,
passing new legislation.

[4]

§ 2–2. Legislative initiative through words.
Those who propose actual words contribute most
of the initiative for legislative policy. Words
come into the process in two ways, in draft bills as
introduced and as amendments to bills. An idea
becomes an item of legislative business when
someone turns it into a bill. Bills provide the
basis for the legislative work of deciding public
policy. Making a bill, from idea conception to
first draft to "for introduction" version, is difficult intellectual labor. It is so challenging, in
fact, that it deters from action most of those who
have a desire to petition a legislature.

Changing the words of a bill by amendment is
the means to accomplish two important legislative tasks, accommodation of interested and affected groups and elimination of technical defects. A great part of legislative attention goes
into decisions on amendments rather than into
struggles over whether a bill will be passed or
defeated. The nimble legislator or lobbyist probes
to find word changes which will silence an opponent or turn him into a supporter. Many of the
most important provisions which finally become
law are adjusted by amendments as the legislative machinery works to accommodate conflicting
viewpoints and to reflect in the words of an act the
collective judgment of all those who play a role
in the legislative institution. The citizen who
wants to be among those who "play a role in the

legislature" plays a stronger role when he works with words; that is, when he asks for a specific bill or a specific amendment, when he argues the merits of a particular bill or amendment, when he writes the bill or the amendment, and, most of all, when he thinks up the bill or the amendment.

CHAPTER 2

OPERATION OF A LEGISLATURE

A. THE INSTITUTION

§ 3–1. **Bicameral–unicameral.** The United States Congress and forty-nine state legislatures are organized as bicameral bodies. The Nebraska legislature and most county and municipal legislative institutions are organized on a unicameral basis. A bicameral legislature is really two institutions. The two houses of a legislature have separate procedures and leadership. Joint committees and joint hearings are the exception rather than the rule. Some members of one house may be complete strangers to a member of the other house. This amazes those citizens who reasonably expect legislative work to throw together the few score of individuals who enjoy the status of legislator. But legislative bill-passing efforts are really two conflicts—the battle of the upper house (senate) and the battle of the lower house (assembly).

§ 3–2. **The larger institution.** One reason for the separateness of house and senate is that members represent but a part of the legislative institution. Legislative staff, reporters, lobbyists from private and public entities, and other interested

[7]

citizens swell the ranks of the larger institution to hundreds of persons. To participate effectively in deliberations on an issue in either house requires familiarity with the lobbyists, bureaucrats, citizens, and staff contributing to consideration of the issue in that house. Those players are more important than almost any member of the other house, for each house gives a proposal consideration independent of the other body. The time demands on a legislator who is effectively involved in legislative work in his own house require him to ration his acquaintance-making energies. He may not cross paths with new or inactive members of the other house for weeks or months. He will know lobbyists, reporters, and staff much more quickly.

§ 3–3. **Lobbyists.** A legislative institution is a huge fact-finding and educating machine. Being elected gives an individual a special role in that machine. But the opportunity for other citizens to participate in its work is great, if they act with insight. The hired lobbyist has no credential as he arrives at the legislature, other than that somebody pays him to show up to represent a particular point of view. The citizen who comes on a volunteer basis lacks even that credential. While disinterest and integrity of motive may be asserted as a substitute credential for the volunteer, experienced legislators expect

[8]

more honest and reliable information from hired lobbyists. The unknown volunteer may be a narrow ideologue or may be concealing a significant personal economic interest. To be effective, the volunteer must build trust by presence at the legislature over a period of time and by demonstrating respect for the institution and its members. Hired or volunteer, the lobbyist plays a major role in the legislative institution. He prepares its bills, he prepares amendments to those bills, he advocates bills, he advocates amendments, he develops compromises, and he facilitates communication between the two houses. When a legislator shares decision making with his staff, the lobbyist extends his advocacy to the staff. When public opinion is critical, he provides information to reporters and editorial writers. Lobbyists show up on the field of battle armed with information and often with politically potent constituencies behind them. They are an essential part of the legislative institution.

§ 3–4. Committees. Woodrow Wilson wrote, "The Congress in committee is Congress at work." The work of legislative bodies is done through committees to divide the labor. Nearly every legislative action follows a committee recommendation. That recommendation is reported to the floor of the house, confirmed by floor action, and becomes the official action of that house. All bills are not reported to the floor, however.

[*9*]

In most jurisdictions, committees pigeonhole bills which the committee chairman decides to leave off the committee agenda or which are laid over by the committee after hearing.

The autonomy of committees in their decision making varies from institution to institution and from time to time. The degree of autonomy is probably the most significant variable among legislative bodies. It determines to a large extent the amount of control that leadership cliques hold over the work of the institution. Institution-wide leadership always competes with the more decentralized control of the committee chairmen, who often exercise pre-eminent power in the area of their jurisdiction. The degree of committee autonomy also affects the opportunity for legislators to attack problems beyond their own assignments. In some legislative bodies, notably the United States House of Representatives, a legislator can work with real effectiveness only on issues handled in his committees. Even when the issue produces an intense floor fight, members of the committee with jurisdiction will lead the battle on the two sides of the issue. The most powerful legislators, if not members of the committee, must exercise their leadership in backstage roles. Where committee autonomy is not so dominant, legislators are free to sponsor bills before any committee and to participate actively in the floor advocacy on any bill and any amendment.

The role of the committee in the legislative process can hardly be exaggerated. Still, the committee is subject to the consensus of the body. If it is seriously out of step with majority opinion within a house, its decisions will be attacked and reversed. The leadership of the committee will respond by modifying its actions so as to avoid provoking floor rejection of its decisions.

Generally the committee structure of a legislative body is determined by the steering committee of the majority group, although in some jurisdictions and in the United States Congress a statute establishes the structure. Where the pattern of organization is left to each newly elected legislature, the number and jurisdiction of committees varies from session to session. The number often depends on how many members are eligible for committee chairmanships on the basis of seniority; for example, a committee may be established for each majority caucus member serving at least his third term. The jurisdiction of committees may be adjusted to fit the talent and ambition of the various chairmen. Strong chairmen expand the variety and significance of bills referred to their committees at the expense of less assertive chairmen. When there are jurisdictional disputes, legislative leaders direct bills to preferred committees, usually to a committee chaired with a steady hand by an established member of the body's hierarchy.

§ 3–5. Subcommittees. The labor of the institution may be further divided through the use of subcommittees. Subcommittees may be standing subcommittees to deal with particular subject areas or *ad hoc* subcommittees to deal with specific bills. Sometimes subcommittees are used as a repository for bills which the committee or committee chairman do not wish to be bothered with again. More commonly, subcommittees are used to do the hard work of taking testimony, redrafting language, and developing the compromises necessary before a bill is submitted to the full committee and to the floor.

One measure of the need for division of labor in legislatures is a reverse relationship between the number of standing committees and the number of subcommittees. Inevitably, the fewer the standing committees, the more numerous are policy-making subcommittees. A commonly suggested change in structure is to reduce the number of standing committees so the assignments of each legislator can be reduced. This recommendation fails to take into account the phenomenon of multiplying subcommittees. It also ignores the fact that as the number of committees is reduced, each surviving committee carries a heavier work load, for it must cover two or three subject areas and consider more bills.

The most efficient division of legislative resources occurs instead with more numerous, but *small* standing committees. First, this reduces the occasions on which policy-making battles occur at the subcommittee level only to be duplicated in the full committee. Second, having fewer members on each committee reduces the number of assignments of each legislator. Third, these reduced assignments are to committees which do not cover such broad jurisdictions.

Often policy-making subcommittees are duplicative and time wasting, but this criticism is not applicable to small subcommittees which polish a bill prior to full committee consideration. Such work-horse subcommittees save legislative energy by sharpening the issues, screening out avoidable conflicts, and inserting perfecting amendments.

§ 3–6. Leadership. Leadership in a legislative body is profoundly affected by the committee structure of that body. To understand a legislative institution, the interrelationships of its formal leaders—speaker, majority leader, minority leader, president, caucus steering committees and committee chairmen—must be analyzed. To influence the product it is essential to know who makes what decisions. On some issues and in some legislatures it is a small, dominant clique of majority caucus leaders. In other institutions, decisions are made by committee chairmen and their supporters; the formal legislative leadership plays a housekeeping and coordinating role. Even where the legislative committee is quite autonomous, there are decisions on which leaders gauge the consensus of the house and the public and communicate it to the committee. On these issues the committee structure serves largely to rubber-stamp leadership decisions and, within the parameters of those decisions, to polish and flesh out the bill.

Generally, the larger a legislative body, the more centralized the leadership. This makes the speaker of the assembly the dominant single legislator in most jurisdictions. He and the assembly majority leader often serve as a team, overseeing the committee work of the assembly and stepping in with directions on the substance of legislation on key issues. Senates are more apt to be organized as an oligarchy of committee chairmen because of their smaller size and the longer service of members. The longer the service, the more automatic are the prerogatives of a legislator. This reduces the leverage available to the formally elected legislative leaders. Legislative leadership is generally carried out by persuasion rather than command. But on the continuum between polite requests and orders, the spot at which a particular house operates is determined by the stability of committee leadership and membership.

The organization of a legislature consists of a formal committee structure and the elected lead-

ership of the body as a whole and of its separate
political caucuses. This formal apportionment of
power within the institution is adjusted in a variety of ways, especially to account for the extra,
informal influence of members with extraordinary
ability and personality. The legislator who holds
a particular title may exercise the power that
should go with the title. On the other hand, the
possessor of the title may be so deferential to the
opinions of other members that lobbying efforts
intended to influence his actions are most effectively channeled through more dominant members. A common mistake in dealing with legislative institutions is to assume the power of the
institution coincides with the formal titles rather
than to examine the real life relationships and
lines of power within the institution.

§ 3–7. **Legislative norms.** Overlying formal
legislative structure and official rules of procedure
and organization are patterns of behavior or legislative norms. These unwritten rules vary from
institution to institution and from time to time,
but the following are universally present to some
degree. These norms are drawn from the Jewell
and Patterson study, *The Legislative Process in
the United States*.

(a) Legislative work. Legislators are rewarded with expanded influence in the institution as
they work at the task of being a legislator. Legis-

lators who demonstrate interest in personal advancement or publicity rather than in the quality of the legislative product lose some legislative influence, even if their non-legislative political power grows.

(b) Specialization. Legislators are expected to concentrate their energies in a limited number of fields, demonstrating an understanding of the necessity for division of labor and the prerogatives of other members who carry responsibility for decision-making in different fields. The legislator who flits from issue to issue is usually a dilettante and is soon recognized as such.

(c) Institutional patriotism. A legislator is expected to respect his institution. He demonstrates that respect by working at his job and by behaving in other ways which contribute to the esteem in which it is held by the public. Occasionally the issue of institutional loyalty arises in power clashes between the executive and the legislative branch. When the issue is perceived as a matter of legislative prerogatives, the legislator who sides with the executive rather than with his own institution loses influence.

(d) Party loyalty. Loyalty is a political commodity of high value and legislatures are political institutions. Therefore, the pressure of party caucus loyalty is significant. The degree to which party discipline is asserted in legislative bodies varies, but when an issue arises in which the majority of a caucus asserts a party position and requests all members of that caucus to stay in line, acceptance of the request is expected. To stray is excused, however, when the legislator's constituency is antagonistic to the caucus position or when he is already on record on the other side of the issue.

(e) Reciprocity. Legislators are expected to help one another. This involves geographic and ideologic tolerance. The legislator who approaches each issue with the narrow viewpoint of what it will do for him and for his constituency, ignoring broader interests and ignoring the political imperatives facing his colleagues, finds himself out of step with the spirit of the institution. He also finds himself short of accumulated goodwill when he faces a legislative situation in which he needs the broad-minded understanding of his colleagues.

(f) Interpersonal courtesy. Goodwill among members of the legislature increases the capacity of the institution to do its work effectively. Facing a multitude of conflicts—some bitter—a legislative institution can be torn apart by personal animosities. To protect against this development, the norm in legislatures is to separate personalities from issues. Motives of members are not questioned. Debate is carried on in the most impersonal and respectful of terms. When debate on

[*17*]

an issue is concluded, that conflict is forgotten and the body turns to its next task with a minimum of retained rancor. The vernacular is "disagree without being disagreeable."

Some unwritten rules conflict directly with the written rules of the institution. For example, written rules always authorize a motion to close off debate, but unwritten norms of many state legislatures dictate that the motion is never made. The rules of a legislature may authorize unlimited co-sponsorship on bills, but custom may dictate that sponsors are held to a low number.

§ 3–8. Seniority. One legislative norm is universally applied. That is the rule of seniority. In any legislative institution, newcomers serve an apprenticeship in which they learn the written and unwritten rules of the institution and develop some specialization through their committee assignments. Members who return for second, third, and subsequent terms are favored with assignment to more preferred committees, or at least are allowed to retain assignments of prior sessions. The strictness with which seniority is applied varies from legislature to legislature, but in all it is followed to a significant extent. The seniority system earned a bad name through slavish adherence to it in the United States Congress. The evils in the pre-1975 congressional system should not be imputed to state legislatures,

[*18*]

however. Because state legislators are closer to home and exposed to their constituencies on a more regular basis, because turnover in state legislatures is much greater than in Congress, because the perquisites of office are fewer and the temptation to hold on to the office tenaciously is therefore less, the incidence of senility in state legislative committee chairmen is lower than in congressional committees. Turnover of membership causes a less rigid adherence to the seniority system in state legislatures, so weaker members are usually side-tracked into chairmanships of minor committees.

The seniority system as utilized by most legislatures is justified. Its justification lies partly in recognizing experience and the sounder judgments of maturity. An even more valid justification is that seniority avoids fratricide within the legislative body. Any method of assigning committee memberships and chairmanships less cut-and-dried than seniority opens the door to factionalism, political maneuver, vote-trading, resentment, and a disintegration of discipline and order. Seniority is retained in the process of legislative organization because it is the only way to avoid problems much greater than the problems of seniority itself. It is hard to imagine a way to bind up the wounds that would follow a struggle for committee assignments and chairmanships conducted without the restraint of seniority guidelines. Furthermore, whatever problems arise from seniority can be reduced, and generally are, by modifications in the rigidity with which the system is applied. Reducing the opportunities for autocratic behavior by individual committee chairmen—old or young—also can help. The legislative process, which is essentially a consensus procedure, usually operates in a way which counteracts the evils of weak or senile or dictatorial committee chairmen.

B.   INERTIA

§ 4–1. **Acquiescence.** Legislatures are organized to divide and share work loads. The organization is also designed to build consensus from which decisions emerge. Division of labor cannot occur without acquiescence by members in the decisions made by the committees or subcommittees to which primary responsibility for various policy making is assigned. Consensus cannot develop unless individual viewpoints are submerged or adjusted so as not to interfere with finding a common ground upon which group agreement can be built.

The most frequent legislator decision is to go along—to acquiesce—in decisions made by others. Acquiescence includes supporting subcommittees and committees, not offering amendments, not speaking, not raising alternatives or questions,

[*20*]

accepting compromises already made. Going along is usually easy, for the legislator lacks information to support a dissent. Sometimes going along requires great restraint when he has information and therefore a reason to object. A legislator's decision then must take into account the continued effectiveness of the division of labor provided by the committee structure. If a legislature habitually overturns committee work, each legislator faces more and more decisions as he sits in his body's chamber in floor session. There he has no help from specialization, from hearings, from extensive discussion, from thinking time, or from between-meeting compromises. This makes the leadership plea to uphold the system of divided labor and responsibility most persuasive. The argument is not for the particular decision, but for the system.

Each legislator has two other reasons for supporting committee decisions. First, he does committee work himself which he wants respected and accepted. If he successfully undercuts other committees, his committees become less sovereign. Second, his acceptance by other legislators depends on playing by the rules, including the rule of accommodation and the rule of respect for conflicting viewpoints.

§ 4–2. **Inertia.** Inertia is a law of physics defined as "the tendency of matter to remain at rest, if at rest, or, if moving, to keep moving in the same direction unless affected by some outside force." Inertia is a universal characteristic of legislative institutions, just as it is universal in our physical world. Its two aspects, inertness and momentum, serve to describe and explain legislatures better than any other analogy.

Legislatures are organized to keep unnecessary or deleterious bills bottled up where they will not consume legislative energy. Committees are expected to hold a bill until its sponsors meet a significantly difficult burden of persuasion. A bill stays pigeonholed and "at rest" in a committee unless outside forces provide the push to get it moving.

When public demand, skilled lobbying, or an effective sponsor (and the merits of the proposal) start a bill moving, legislators usually allow the bill to continue forward in its initial thrust. They accept early decisions of draftsmen, sponsors, subcommittees and committees. Unless someone steps forward with an amendment and with information supporting his suggestion, a proposal may move to passage, as is, propelled primarily by legislative momentum. It will be adopted in a form consistent with the initial bill unless outside forces cause modification.

Legislative procedure is premised on the idea that a bill escapes its initial resting place when a need for the bill has been demonstrated. The presumption then follows that the bill deserves processing at the next step of the procedure and at each step thereafter unless some force prompts the unusual decision along the way to re-evaluate prior affirmative action. As a bill gets closer to passage, it is harder to kill or even to amend; the burden of persuasion for making any change becomes heavier. Energy expended early in the process is therefore much more effective than energy applied late in the process. Early lobbying has another advantage. Fewer members are involved in decisions at the start of the process so the task of persuading the decision makers is less difficult. It can be done by contact with a handful of legislators and before momentum is at work.

C. BILL PASSING MANDATES AND RULES

§ 5–1. **Variability.** The procedure by which legislation is enacted varies from jurisdiction to jurisdiction and from house to house within a jurisdiction. It also varies over time within a house. The following materials therefore must be treated as a general survey and as a foundation for a study of the details of procedure in a specific legislative institution.

§ 5–2. Constitutional mandates. Constitutions, the basic governmental charters, lay down various procedural mandates for legislatures. Typical mandates are that a particular kind of legislation, for example a capital expenditure, requires an extraordinary vote. Three separate readings of bills are commonly required. In some jurisdictions, constitutions provide for reading at length, a requirement which is of necessity circumvented in practice. Constitutions often require the affirmative vote of a majority of all those elected to each house (not just those present) in order to pass a bill. Another requirement may be that the names of those voting *aye* and *nay* be recorded in the journal. Constitutions may prescribe the period during which a legislature's work must be completed. Authority for an executive to veto legislation is constitutionally established and the procedure for vetoing and for overriding may be spelled out in detail. Constitutions may prescribe that certain officers such as speaker and president *pro tem* be elected by legislative bodies and may assign them legislative tasks. One common requirement, not applicable to the United States Congress, is that a bill contain a single subject which must be expressed in its title. This requirement limits the packaging of legislative work and thus significantly affects procedures.

Procedural restrictions imposed by constitutions may or may not be subject to judicial enforcement depending on whether the state follows the journal entry or the enrolled bill rule. (see §§ 41 and 42).

§ 5–3. **Legislative rules.** Rules are adopted in each legislative body to spell out the organization and the procedure of the body. These rules generally include a provision incorporating *Mason's Manual of Legislative Procedure* as the controlling authority for any situation not covered by a specific rule. For the serious student of legislative procedure, *Mason's Manual* is the authoritative source.

Rules adopted by individual legislative bodies usually reflect historical incidents within that house in which the general rules of parliamentary practice led to some difficulty. Afterward, locking the barn door, the body adopts a special rule to prevent repetition of the difficulty. Some rules provide special procedures for modifying the general rules of parliamentary practice; other rules simply reaffirm the ordinary parliamentary practices and place them in the rules of the body so they will not be overlooked by the newly initiated. Legislatures frequently need to depart from regular order to do essential work. Therefore, the rule for suspension of the rules is used so often that it is an integral part of normal procedure.

[25]

A rules suspension requires a two-thirds vote, so minorities are protected from unfair or unexpected departures from regular procedures.

Procedures involving both houses of a bicameral legislature may be included in joint rules adopted by both or may be adopted in the separate rules of each house.

§ 5–4. **Resolutions.** Some legislative work is done through joint, concurrent, assembly, or senate resolutions, rather than through bills. The use of resolutions is largely a matter of custom in any legislative body. Typically a joint resolution is one which originates in one house and with the concurrence of the other house has the force of official legislative action. It is used to propose state constitutional amendments and to ratify federal constitutional amendments. In some jurisdictions a joint resolution may substitute for a bill, if submitted to the executive and signed. A concurrent resolution, like the joint resolution, originates in one house and is concurred in by the other. It does not have the legal impact of a joint resolution. It is more commonly used as a means of expressing opinion on some issue. Petitions from state legislatures to the federal Congress or President are drawn as concurrent resolutions. Commendations to statesmen and winning basketball teams are further examples of concurrent resolutions.

A senate or assembly resolution is used to accomplish internal housekeeping of the body. Most things accomplished through a one-house resolution could be accomplished by motion, but a resolution is used for greater formality. For example, resolutions are used to adopt the rules of the house, to establish committees, to initiate investigations, to authorize and hire employees. The day-to-day work of the body is conducted through simple floor motions.

D. TYPICAL HURDLES IN ONE HOUSE

§ 6–1. A bill for an act. With the warning—repeated—that legislative procedure varies from institution to institution and from time to time, the following sections describe typical steps a bill must follow in a legislative body. Technical and tactical considerations are discussed for each of these steps.

The official legislative process starts and ends with a bill for an act. From the moment of introduction to final approval, all procedures of the institution focus on a bill. The significance of this concentration cannot be overstated. Having a specific bill under consideration forces a legislature to face issues directly rather than to engage in philosophical debates. The decision-making process of legislative bodies has a crispness superior to that of most other group-led institutions. Focusing on a written proposal in the form of a bill for an act is primarily responsible for this characteristic.

§ 6–2. Obtaining sponsors.

A bill is introduced into the legislative machine through the sponsorship of an elected member. Rules may allow a limited or unlimited number of co-sponsors on a proposal. It is advantageous to obtain co-sponsors who provide political, geographic, and ideological balance, since balanced sponsorship reduces the suspicion with which a bill is examined. The chief author or sponsor is the legislator who manages the bill as it passes through the institution. He makes tactical decisions and carries a heavy responsibility of explanation and advocacy in committee and on the floor. Legislators in the majority caucus with special talent for managing legislation are beseiged with requests to handle bills. Knowledgeable lobbyists choose chief sponsors with utmost care, for the wrong sponsor can seriously handicap a bill's progress. It is efficient and effective to seek as chief sponsor a member of the committee with jurisdiction over the bill. Co-sponsors from the same committee are also advantageous, because each sponsor is somewhat committed to cast an affirmative vote in committee. Starting with three, four, or five semi-secure affirmative committee votes is extremely helpful. Even when a committee member turns down a request to sponsor or co-sponsor a bill, the time spent explaining the bill to him may pay off later when the committee considers the measure. The request to sponsor a bill provides an early opportunity to present the bill's merits.

§ 6–3. **Introduction of bill.** After the chief sponsor's and co-sponsors' names are signed on a bill, it is ready for introduction. Introduction may be a routine matter or may involve a number of tactical decisions. Some bills are introduced on slow news days and are accompanied by press releases with the hope of attracting news coverage. Other bills are saved for times when the bill will receive a minimum of attention. The decision depends on whether the sponsors feel public opinion is more likely to work for or against the bill.

At the time of introduction the bill is referred to a standing committee. Sponsors of the bill, when there is room for judgment on the reference, attempt to arrange with the speaker, the president of the senate, the parliamentarian, or other ministerial officer for reference to the desired committee. In most legislatures, committee jurisdiction is so flexible that the proper reference is not cut-and-dried. In the case of major legislation, reference to two or more committees may be required; then which committee gets the bill on first reference may be of critical importance.

§ 6–4. Committee action. When a bill has been introduced and referred to a committee, the task of its advocates is to win a place on the committee agenda and then to obtain a favorable committee recommendation. Committee agendas are largely controlled by the committee chairman, so the conventional view is of autocratic committee chairmen deciding which bills will be passed and which will be pigeonholed. This view is not without validity, but group consensus plays a significant role in committee agenda making, as it does throughout the legislative process. A committee chairman does not maintain the committee members' allegiance and the highest degree of effectiveness by disregarding committee attitudes on what ought to be scheduled. Therefore, the most dictatorial-appearing decisions of committee chairmen usually are consensus decisions from the committee itself or from the majority members and caucus leaders. Other legislators hide behind the chairman.

Nonetheless, the campaign for a spot on the committee agenda is appropriately directed toward the chairman and his staff. The competition for committee time is intense. Bills heard are essential, or popular, or generally beneficial, or noncontroversial, or particularly appealing to the committee chairman. Sometimes a bill is scheduled mainly to head off a more obnoxious proposal. If a spot cannot be won on the committee agenda, proponents of a bill may request subcommittee consideration. In subcommittee, a partially developed proposal can be polished into a solid draft which then wins a spot on the full committee agenda.

The heaviest lobbying on a bill is conducted while it rests in committee because the legislative system of division of labor makes the committee decision the decision of the whole body. If that decision is for inaction (laying over or pigeonholing), the bill is effectively stopped for that session of the legislature. If the committee recommends that the bill be formally killed (indefinitely postponed), that recommendation is reported to the floor as a committee report to be confirmed by house vote. Adoption of the committee report officially kills the bill.

If the committee recommends passage of the bill, it is sent to the floor with a favorable committee report. This recommendation carries the bill past the major obstacle in the legislative process. Committees keep from the floor, and from passage, the great mass of proposals. Therefore, an affirmative committee recommendation is the greatest single forward step in the process.

Some bills include provisions within the jurisdiction of more than one committee. The first committee then must re-refer the bill to another for further consideration. Although the second committee may kill a bill, the momentum provided by the first affirmative recommendation puts pressure on it to act favorably. The second committee may by amendment water down the bill but is reluctant to directly challenge another committee's recommendation that the bill be passed.

§ 6–5. **Re-referral.** After the legislative body adopts a committee recommendation that a bill pass, the bill is placed on the agenda for floor action. That agenda may be long. During its wait for floor action, and at any time until final passage, a bill is subject to a motion to re-refer it to the committee which recommended it or to some other committee. The tactic of re-referral, since it avoids a direct decision on the merits and pushes the bill back behind the great obstacle of committee approval, is a favorite for opponents. From the proponents' perspective, the motion to re-refer is dangerous for three reasons. First, opponents control the timing of the motion so it will be made when it is most likely to prevail; that is when either through absences, events, or concentrated lobbying the bill's opponents are strongest. Second, a *prima facie* case of inadequate committee consideration can be made on behalf of a re-referral motion against any bill because of the time pressures under which legislatures work. Third, a basic principle of legislative tactics is to seek the softest method of accomplishing an objective.   The motion to re-refer is the classic example of the gentle but deadly motion.   It is much easier for legislators to vote to re-refer a bill than to cast a hard negative vote on final passage.   The re-referral vote is cloaked in procedural or right-to-be-heard camouflage; there is ambiguity in the motion to send a bill back to a committee for interminable further consideration.

§ 6–6.   **Committee of the whole.**   In most state legislatures, the first floor consideration of a bill occurs in committee of the whole.   This means an entire house sits as a committee to consider the bill.   The historical foundation of the committee of the whole procedure was the desire of early parliaments to act on legislation in semi-secrecy, without recorded votes, and thus to be independent of the king's sanctions.   The committee of the whole has survived partly to give legislators an opportunity to act on bills free of the political consequences of recorded votes.   More basically it provides an opportunity for less formal debate without limitations on the duration or number of times a member may speak.   Preliminary consideration of a bill in committee of the whole also provides an interval between first floor consideration and final passage. This interval gives an opportunity for reflection on the debate and on the bill. The effect is more careful consideration.

For better or worse, use of comittee of the whole procedure is declining. Increasingly bills are taken up for debate and amendment, then put immediately to final vote while the subject is fresh in members' minds. Moves toward openness in government have put the unrecorded vote in disrepute, although the committee of the whole may be used with recorded votes. Time pressures make separate committee of the whole consideration a burden which must be balanced against the benefits of a more deliberative procedure.

§ 6–7. Alternatives to committee of the whole.

A body may omit use of the committee of the whole practice for selected types of bills, for special circumstances, or totally. In almost every legislature there exists a consent calendar procedure to be followed for bills identified by committee reports as noncontroversial. The consent calendar is taken up at a designated time, each bill is briefly explained and voted on, and then the next bill is taken up for a similarly brief explanation and vote. If even two or three members of the body object to a bill on a consent calendar, their objections bump the bill back to a regular calendar for more careful examination. The consent calendar device permits a legislative body to dispose of many minor bills with a minimum of energy.

Another set of bills likely to bypass the committee of the whole procedure are the major bills which legislative leadership wishes to process with a tighter rein than is possible in committee of the whole, where votes may be unrecorded and attendance somewhat unpredictable. The device used for processing these major bills is some variety of special order or special rule by which the bill is specially scheduled for debate, amendment, and passage at a single session. The designation of a bill for special order is accomplished in a variety of ways. Sometimes an extraordinary majority (two-thirds) of the body designates bills for special order. More commonly, selecting bills for special order treatment is delegated to a majority caucus policy committee, to the bipartisan leadership of the body, or to a priority setting committee as described in the next section. Bills from appropriations and tax committees may get automatic special order privileges because they must pass and usually are reported out of committee near adjournment deadlines.

§ 6–8. Priority setting committees. In some legislative bodies, standing committees regularly report to the floor more bills than the body has time to consider. In this situation machinery must be established to pick out bills for floor consideration and to leave other bills to die with adjournment.   The machinery usually established is a priority setting committee, the most famous of which is the Rules committee of the United States House of Representatives.   This committee may designate for priority consideration any bill reported to the floor of the House by another committee.   Bills adopted by the House of Representatives reach final passage either through a consent calendar procedure, through a two-thirds vote suspending the rules, or by Rules committee action.   Since mustering a two-thirds suspension-of-the-rules vote is an impossibility for any measure with substantial opposition, the major pieces of national legislation must pass through the House Rules committee.   This is the key to its great power.   In the United States Senate, with less intense time pressure, priority setting is the task of the majority party policy committee.   In practice, floor agendas are usually set by agreement between the majority and minority leaders and reflect a consensus of the entire Senate.

The devices used in state legislatures are generally some variety of special order procedure, a variation on the House Rules committee procedure, or an informal consensus device similar to that of the United States Senate.

§ 6–9. **Final passage.**   Under a few constitutions, including that of the United States, a vote on final passage may be oral and unrecorded un-

less the *ayes* and *nays* are called for by a member
of the body. A call for the *ayes* and *nays* is ordi-
narily a right on any motion and invariably is a
right on final passage. In many states the constitution requires that a bill must receive an affirmative vote from a majority of all members to
pass and that the votes must be recorded in the
journal. Since previous steps of the process usually require only a simple majority of those voting
on the question, the final vote is the highest formal
hurdle. However, by the time a bill has reached
this point in the process, accommodations have
been made with some of those in opposition, and
on most bills there is such momentum that defeat
on final passage is rare.

The vote on final passage may be reconsidered
for a limited period of time. When the vote is
close, those on the losing side look for converts
among those on the prevailing side. If vote
switches are found, a motion to reconsider may
succeed. Occasionally the makers of a motion to
reconsider are surprised by the loss of some of
their own supporters; in a situation where reconsideration is likely, the winners as well as the
losers look for members with whom some additional advocacy may be effective. The number
of successful reconsiderations is not substantial,
but it is a device which occasionally proves useful
in opening the door for additional compromise to
accommodate the interests of groups competing

on an issue. Generally, rules permit reconsideration of any vote only once. Therefore, when those on the losing side seem likely to move to reconsider, those on the prevailing side may ask that the vote be reconsidered immediately and urge that the motion be defeated. If the motion is defeated, the losing side is precluded from moving to reconsider at a later time (after a campaign to change votes). In the United States Congress the motion to reconsider is routinely made and laid on the table to give finality to votes.

E. THE OTHER HOUSE AND THE EXECUTIVE

§ 7–1. **Agreement.** In a bicameral legislature, passage of a bill by one house carries the bill a significant way toward passage. Passage by the first house usually makes affirmative action by the second substantially easier to achieve. Reasons for this include: the bill requires less work in the second house since rough edges have been removed by the first; opponents have had input in the first house and, if accommodated there, may hold their fire as the bill is processed in the second; inter-house relationships may be improved by passage of the bill and harmed by its rejection; and concern about wasting time on a bill that will not pass is reduced since the bill has already cleared the other house. There also exists a

[*38*]

momentum—legislative inertia—from previous affirmative action. Members of the second house assume the affirmative vote in the first house had a basis in logic. Thus some of the burden of persuasion shifts to the negative side.

After the final affirmative vote for passage by the first house, the bill is put into an official engrossment and transmitted to the other house for consideration. Each house must act on the same document. Therefore, if the senate acts on a bill first, the senate bill becomes the subject of consideration in the assembly. If the assembly acts first, its bill becomes the object of consideration in the senate. Some procedure is provided for advancing on the agenda any bill from the other house if its parallel or companion bill has had any formal action. An assembly bill will be substituted for the companion senate bill on the senate committee of the whole calendar, for example.

If the house giving second consideration to the bill accepts the version adopted by the first house, it returns the bill with a message so indicating. The first house then enrolls the bill, obtains the signatures of the officers of the two houses, and transmits the bill to the executive for his signature. If the second house has amended the bill, the message returning the bill requests concurrence in those amendments. Sponsors of the bill in the first house, consulting with interested lobbyists, committee chairmen, and other legislators, determine whether the other body's amendments are acceptable. If so, a motion is made to concur in the amendments and to place the bill on repassage. If the motion passes, the formalities of a final vote are repeated for the bill in its amended form. This means again recording the *ayes* and *nays* if required by the constitution. If repasssed, the bill is enrolled in its amended form, signed by the legislative officers, and transmitted to the executive for his signature.

If the house of origin refuses to concur in the amendments of the second house, the complex conference committee procedure described in the next section is used to resolve the differences between the two houses.

§ 7–2. Disagreement; conference committees. The mechanism for compromising differences between senate and assembly is a conference committee. It usually consists of three to five members from each house named after each body adopts a motion calling for the conference. The speaker generally names assembly conferees, after consultation with chairmen of relevant committees and minority leadership. In senates the appointment is likely to be made by a policy committee or a committee on committees encompassing the senate leadership. Bill authors and leaders on the committee which processed the bill are given priority in conference committee selections.

After their selection the two delegations sit down together, choose a chairman from their membership, note the differences between the two versions of the bill before the conference, dispose of secondary issues involving minor differences, and then, through give-and-take, resolve the significant policy differences.

In state legislatures the members representing each body are expected to uphold the position of their house against the contrary position of the other house. In Congress minority party members must be included as conferees from both houses. This statutory requirement occasionally leads to the incongruous situation of the minority membership from both houses uniting with the majority membership of one house to dictate terms of the conference report. In all bodies, conference committee members regularly suffer the discomfort of conflicting obligations. It is not unusual for a senate conferee to prefer an assembly position, for his party caucus to prefer the assembly position, or for his constituency to be better served by the other version. In these circumstances he will be a soft conferee, eager to compromise and less than vigorous in his advocacy.

In a conference, as is true throughout the legislative process, there is more effort to discover and willingness to accept the merits of opposing positions than is generally realized by those who have not had close contact with legislative institutions. Differences are generally resolved after discussion of the merits. Even if the compromise is splitting-the-difference, this amounts to averaging the values of the assembly and senate so as to reflect the judgment of the whole institution.

Once the differences are resolved, a conference committee report is prepared for submission to the two houses. The committee report goes first to the house which initially passed the bill. If the report is adopted, the bill is placed on repassage in its compromise form. After the final vote is taken, the conference committee report and the bill are sent to the other house where again the report of the conference committee is submitted for approval and, when the report is approved, the bill placed on repassage. After repassage, the bill is returned to the house of origin, enrolled, signed by the officers of the legislature, and submitted to the executive for his signature.

A conference committee may be allowed to deal generally with the subject matter before it or it may be limited to resolving the differences between the two houses. Even where the conference committee is not by rule limited in its jurisdiction, legislative custom severely limits the freedom with which new subject matter can be inserted into the conference bill. But occasionally a conference committee produces unexpected results beyond its mandate. These excursions occur even where the rules impose strict limitations on conference committee jurisdiction. This is symptomatic of the authoritarian power of conference committees. Conference reports are returned to assembly and senate on a take-it-or-leave-it basis, and the bodies are generally placed in the position so that to leave-it is a practical impossibility. Conference committees are the most undemocratic procedure in the legislative process, and appropriate targets for legislative critics. But they are essential in a bicameral system; the only way to eliminate them is to substitute the unicameral for the bicameral system. Short of this far-reaching change, the conference committee is an evil which must be endured.

§ 7-3. Veto or signature. The final step in the legislative process is the signature on an enrolled bill by the executive and his filing of the act with the secretary of state. When an executive declines to sign a bill, he may return it to the legislature with a veto message explaining the reasons for his disapproval. With the house of origin acting first, the legislature may attempt to override the veto by an extraordinary vote of each house (usually two-thirds). Some state constitutions provide that the governor may select particular items from appropriation bills for item veto. In these cases his veto message identifies the disapproved items, and the opportunity to override exists on each item. If the governor does not return a bill to the legislature with his formal disapproval, it becomes law without his signature after a specified number of days. The executive deposits the bill in the secretary of state's office and the fact that it became law without the executive's signature is duly noted. When the legislature adjourns before the time for signature runs out, the adjournment prevents the executive from returning the bill with a veto message. Since the executive's time for consideration has been cut short, he is permitted to kill the bill by inaction, a "pocket" veto.

The executive's veto power gives him a central role in the legislative process, if he chooses to assert himself. For example, using the veto threat, he can force amendments which would otherwise be unacceptable to the legislature. The extent to which this power is used varies greatly, depending on the personality of the executive, the political allegiances of the houses, the custom in the jurisdiction, the political independence of the legislators, and the quality of legislative performance. If a legislative body is doing quality work, reflective of popular opinion, and the legislators hold significant political independence in their home constituencies, a governor runs political risks with each veto cast. Furthermore, the legis-

lature has retaliatory power through appropriations, appropriation riders, and a variety of other
devices. Therefore, the great power of the veto
is used cautiously by most executives.

§ 7–4. **Same bill document.** A single document must be passed by both houses and signed
by the governor. Passage by each house is veri-
fied by the signature of its presiding officer and
its chief clerical official. These signatures must
go on the enrolled act before that document is
ready for the executive's signature. If the houses
pass identical but separate bills, the action is
without effect. One of the houses must approve
the official bill document from the other house.

CHAPTER 3

ADVOCACY IN THE LEGISLATURE

A. TO MOVE THE LEGISLATURE

§ 8–1. Education and persuasion. Legislative advocacy is an educational process. Legislators are generalists forced to make policy decisions on thousands of questions each legislative session. They are guided by their general education, their common sense, their instincts, their biases, and the information and advice brought to them by community spokesmen. A legislator spends most of his time gathering information upon which to base his decisions. Legislative advocacy (providing information) occurs at many times and locations: at campaign meetings, at endorsement screening committees, at trade association conventions, at interest group dinners, in governors' offices, in attorney generals' offices, in party platform committees, in offices and lobbies of capitol buildings, and as the constituent composes a letter. Legislative advocacy occurs wherever a legislator or legislative staff member can be addressed directly or indirectly with facts, with logic, with opinion, with suggestions, with entreaties.

While there may be a best time and place for most things, the only general rule about lobbying is to adjust to circumstances. With some legislators on some issues, the best move is to step forward just before he is to vote and give him a relaxed question like: "You don't need any more information supporting our bill, do you? We haven't run across serious problems yet." On some occasions even that approach is too much; it is best to let legislative inertial force carry the bill along.

With other legislators and other issues, lobbying may require contacts long before the legislature convenes. The outcome may depend on dislodging old biases and conventional wisdom, which takes time. Often the earliest lobbying effort is to ask a legislator to sponsor the bill. With major legislation the commitment to manage the bill means a promise to expend many hours of time on that issue at the expense of other responsibilities. For a legislator to make that promise requires deliberation. Many effective legislators make such extensive work commitments before a session starts that to undertake any additional projects later on is impractical; therefore a lobbyist must be early with his request for sponsorship.

Since most legislatures work under constitutional limits on meeting periods and since these limits create severe time pressures during sessions, lobbyists use non-session periods for basic educational efforts. They sow ideas in the off season and reap legislation in due time. However, legislators have other careers which demand their attention when the legislature is not in session. They often want to be left alone when they are away from the capitol, so only compelling and complex issues should be forced upon them then. Requests for attention at any time, but especially during non-session time, must be carefully presented to insure a willing and open-minded listener. Lobbying in the off season, more than lobbying during a session, seeks to educate rather than to win a commitment on how a vote will be cast. Circumstances, including the words of a bill, change; the responsible legislator usually wants to be free to adjust to new circumstances and to influence new words. He is unlikely to commit himself early if there is actual doubt about how he will vote. He is also likely to resent being pushed for a commitment.

Demanding a firm promise is rarely the best method to win a legislator's vote. But it may be essential to get a vote count in order to choose between a bold push for passage or a drastic amendment to salvage part of an otherwise lost cause. Lobbying technique depends in other important ways upon the character and personality of the legislator. Some legislators relish all the attention they can get. Since they do not resent impositions on their time, the lobbyist can urge his cause early and often. Other legislators place high value on their time and resent a second explanation. Some want explanations in writing to allow for homework and staff analysis. Some legislators want quick explanations; some want the merits presented; some want a tally of groups supporting and opposing the action; some want to squeeze in their own amendments; some want only to know the issue is coming up so they can at their leisure recall memories of the pros and cons from past debates and reflect on them. Some listen politely, but burn slowly as the explanation drags; others appear brusk, but appreciate full explanations. Clearly, the lobbyist who knows the members well can adjust his lobbying to the circumstances much better than the drop-in lobbyist. This is just one reason lobbying is one of the most specialized fields among practicing lawyers. (The failure of most lawyers to recognize that their clients have legislative problems is a more distressing reason for the specialization.)

§ 8–2. **Committee hearing.** Legislators spend a great percentage of their time at committee hearings. Cynics sometimes suggest that decisions are cut-and-dried and that hearings are window dressing. But legislators are too busy to spend a significant percentage of their time in any activity which is mere show. Committee hearings, in fact, provide a decision-making forum of utmost importance. The give and take of questioning provides the opportunity to test information in an adversary procedure. Legislators spend more time in hearings and less time reading than is efficient, but politician-legislators commonly are extroverts. The group situation of a committee meeting is more enjoyable to most of them than lonely closed-door study at office or home. Also no one watches homework being done, so more political points are scored in the public arena of the committee hearing. If a politician is at work (learning), he likes to have someone watching.

Formal legislative advocacy is concentrated at committee hearings. They give the legislative advocate his one official opportunity to confront the decision makers with his arguments for or against a bill and for or against amendments to the proposal. The advocate may have opportunities to fill out his story and respond to questions from committee members in less formal circumstances between meetings, however.

Legislative committee meetings vary greatly in purpose and style. On major legislation, committee action usually starts with a hearing at which statements are presented to inform the committee members and to educate the public through press reports of the meeting. The committee carefully accords proponents and opponents equal time. After appropriate hearings, the committee meets at mark-up sessions, where members discuss the issues and adopt amendments to prepare the bill for floor consideration. In some legislatures, formal reports are written which include narrative explanation of the committee action. It is more common in state legislatures to report only the officially approved amendments and the recommendation that the bill pass.

On routine bills or in legislatures with more informal practices, the committee meeting procedure is less structured. Public testimony, action on amendments, committee discussion, and final committee approval or disapproval of the proposal are mixed together and piled on top of each other. Fast-moving committees require a lobbyist to think and act quickly and to be so well prepared that he can cope with unexpected developments.

Some committee hearings, especially in Congress, are designed to build a written record. That record may seek to justify a policy judgment already made, or it may be designed to provide background materials to scholars and others interested in the problem so that legislative solutions to the problem can be constructed.

§ 8–3. **Societal pressure.** A part of legislative advocacy is communicating a sense of the pressures for legislative action present in the community. In the evolution of public knowledge and opinion, a time may come when the pressure for specific legislation is irresistible. Thus in the

[51]

decade beginning in 1910, almost all state legislatures adopted workmen's compensation laws. For a half-century before 1910, the idea of workmen's compensation was gathering academic, business, and social support. Yet the political force to produce legislative action did not mature until New York and Wisconsin acted within a few months of each other. Then the tide for workmen's compensation legislation immediately swept through most of the country. Writings by scholars, journalists, and judges had convinced the public and workers and employers that workmen's compensation programs made sense. Once two states broke the ice without disastrous consequences, the pressures from society to reform compensation to victims of industrial accidents made action a legislative certainty.

The opinion molder who builds perception of a need for legislation is a legislative advocate, even if he does not come to the legislature himself. But the legislative response will be more prompt if perception of a problem is followed quickly by the drafting of proposed legislation and by the presentation of the idea in the form of a bill. The improvement of our society lags tragically because creative individuals fail to convert their good (and brilliant) theories into concrete legislative proposals and to present those proposals to legislatures. There is a break in the communication

[52]

line from the people who have new ideas to those who work in the marble chambers of capitols.

§ 8–4. Persuasion by members. Popular folklore about legislatures includes a dominant leader calling in other legislators and with smile, frown, heavy handshake, backslap, or bearhug passing the word as to how a vote is to be cast. This scene is not drawn entirely from fiction. Legislative leaders with dominating personalities do exist. The impact of the aggressive, self-confident personality upon the legislative institution is no different from the effect of that personality on other institutions. He does produce decision, movement, action. Another personality type with apparently strong impact on legislative performance is the charming leader who whistles his way through legislative tasks like the Pied Piper of Hamelin, picking up a coterie of friends who follow him on many occasions. Legislatures are very human institutions. They respond affirmatively to dominant and charming personalities.

But appearances are deceiving. Individuals who earn reputations for legislative virtuosity are less likely to dominate the institution than to reflect its consensus. In ideology they usually represent the middle ground. They often hold formal leadership positions which give them access to the channels of communication so they can learn the compromise positions where agreement is likely to occur.   Their leadership role may make them messengers to the rest of the body from interest groups such as organized labor, organized agriculture, or the business community.   In this situation they represent less their personal power than their power as agents of campaign financiers and the organized voting blocs of the electorate. Power and political muscle do influence legislative decision making, but it is more the muscle of external pressure groups than the muscle of individual, dominant legislative personalities.   Much more significant in the legislative process than "This is the way it's going to be" is "We've worked out this compromise which we hope is acceptable to you."   The latter statement often follows by a day, week or month the standard question, "What can we do to the bill so you can go along?"

There are other legislators who change the character or direction of decisions in a legislature.   Measured by historical perspectives, their impact may be enormous though they have fewer victories day by day than the consensus-finding leaders.   These legislators may be ahead of the consensus, clearing the way for others to follow. They lead with intellect and courage.   There is significant incompatability between playing the out-front role and being the consensus-finding leader.   The latter uses his reputation for winning as a basic tool.   Occasionally, the roles are combined by an exceptional personality who can communicate to his colleagues which one of his conflicting roles he is playing at different times— captain or pathfinder.

§ 8–5. Ethical standards. Cynicism regarding the competence and the integrity of legislators is widespread. This cynicism is self-defeating because those who expect little from the legislature receive little from it. The citizen who expects decisions on the merits and the interest groups which ask that their cases be fairly and honestly evaluated, usually walk away from the institution impressed by the labor of its members, the openness of its decision making, and its sensitivity to the soundness of the petitions presented. Conscientious legislators everywhere desire that legislative decisions be made independent of extraneous influences that range from the bald corruption of the bribe to the subtle distortions of public policy involved in logrolling and pleas for party loyalty. For the legislator who wants to face each issue on its own merits, the problem is to separate the legitimate legislative function of compromise and accommodation from the ethically objectionable trading of votes and favors. Every legislator faces situations in which political and interpersonal realities make it necessary that he compromise on an issue. It is unrealistic to expect legislatures to be the only institutions in society where friendship, group allegiance, and accommodation play no role. Yet, if too many decisions are made on the basis of accommodation, the price is a legislative institution controlled by favor and entreaty, rather than by fact, logic, and public interest. The standard for member and lobbyist should be to encourage decision on the merits and to refrain from cashing in on friendship and obligation.

B. TACTIC OF SOFTENING ISSUES

§ 9–1. **Easing agreement.** The most basic legislative tactic is to make it as easy as possible to agree with and as difficult as possible to oppose the advocate's position. Each motion is framed to accomplish its objective with the least ruffling of feathers. Drawing sharp lines which precipitate open opposition is avoided. Soft motions increase the temptation to acquiesce, to go along. As a consequence, when a legislator finally makes his most important decisions, each side has usually trimmed its position to a point near mid-ground. Often the difference between victor and loser is hard to discern. The following four sections discuss variations of the issue-softening tactic.

§ 9–2. **Amendment to improve.** The most classic legislative dilemma occurs when either a friend or foe offers an amendment to water down (soften) an objectionable bill. The opponent of the bill intellectually favors whatever will weaken the proposal, but he fears the amendment may moderate the bill just enough to win sufficient votes for passage. He may decide to join supporters of the pure bill to defeat the amendment in the expectation that the pure bill will die. Or he may support the amendment so that if the bill does pass, it will be more acceptable. "Vote for the amendment and against the bill" is a standard instruction from opposition leaders. Either supporters or opponents of the bill may initiate the softening amendment, which complicates the decision on how to vote. For friend and foe, the motion to amend presents the possibility of no loaf, half a loaf, or a full loaf. The decision might be easy if legislative votes could be counted in advance. Almost invariably there are a handful of legislators keeping private counsel on how they intend to vote. This forces sponsors of the bill and leaders of its opposition to make tactical guesses on critical amendments.

A variation on the above dilemma regularly confronts the legislator with a draftsman's pride in the legislative product. He may be presented with a bill whose basic objectives he disapproves but which seems on the way to passage. He may discover a defect in the bill which makes it unworkable or invalid on constitutional grounds. The dilemma is whether to alert sponsors of the proposal to the defect, so the bill may be turned into a technically sound legislative product, or instead to leave the defect in the bill, where it may prove fatal to the sponsors' objective. Working conscientiously on an objectionable proposal is referred to as "building a bridge over the River Kwai."

The dilemma has yet another aspect. A legislator may find a proposal objectionable in general, but abhorrent in some detail. If he asks the sponsors to amend the bill to eliminate the most objectionable provision and they agree, he faces a problem of sportsmanship. Since he has been accommodated, sponsors of the bill resent his vote against passage and will be less likely to accept his subsequent suggestions. There is a general attitude that if a legislator or lobbyist gets his amendment, the bill should get his vote or endorsement. If he is not going to support the bill after winning his amendment, it is important that he tell sponsors in advance that he intends to stay negative even though the amendment is added. Putting the amendment on the bill may still aid proponents, because the opponent may refrain from expressing his opposition. Also the amendment may win over some other legislator.

§ 9–3. Killing with kindness. A bill sometimes is put in jeopardy by amendments which strengthen or expand it. Opponents may attempt to topple it by making the bill top-heavy with amendments, extending its reach beyond politically acceptable limits. The technique is to add provisions to the bill consistent with its main purpose and then shoot it down on the basis of the added provisions. For example, if a little consumer protection is a good thing, a lot of consumer protection may be even better; if a modest subsidy makes sense, a greater subsidy should make more sense. The additions are designed to create enough new opposition or expense to kill the bill.

§ 9–4. **Foot-in-the-door.** Killing with kindness is an effective tactical response to another soft legislative maneuver, the foot-in-the-door technique in which a bill is passed in a limited form to open the way for subsequent legislation. Faced by a small bill with large potential, a legislator is hard put to determine his appropriate course of action. Are the cries that the floodgates are being opened honest or alarmist? Should the bill be evaluated by what appears on its face or for the future? An opponent of the bill, to demonstrate its long range implications, may propose to amend it to a form consistent with its sponsors' ultimate objectives.

A variation of this problem occurs when a bill has precedent-setting potentials. One of the great federal legislative battles of 1972 concerned a guarantee of loans to Lockheed corporation. By congressional standards the money involved was modest, yet the implications of the bill as a precedent in the area of business-government relationships gave it a significance far beyond its own dimensions. The dilemma faced by congressmen on the Lockheed loan legislation is not uncommon. Legislators often first measure short-term pros and cons and then find the debate, and their decision, turning almost entirely on the long-range precedent which will be set if the bill is passed.

§ 9–5. **Compromise.** Legislative compromise is hardly a legislative tactic (some observers view the whole process as compromise), but it does soften an issue. The value of respect for minority viewpoints and the need to accommodate those who have somewhat different goals are well understood in legislatures. As the majority on one issue wins its way and finishes its work, it is replaced by a different majority and a new line-up of votes on another issue. Each time this occurs, tolerance becomes more deeply ingrained in a legislator's character. Allies and opponents change in kaleidoscopic fashion during a legislative session. Therefore, legislatures give dissent a respect it enjoys in few other arenas. There are several classic divisions within a legislature— Democratic versus Republican, liberal versus conservative, labor versus management, rural versus urban, establishment versus young Turk. Each of these splits the body along varying lines on varying subjects and puts a member into alliance and into disagreement with almost every colleague on one or another issue.

Legislative compromise does not enjoy, and does not deserve, an entirely spotless reputation. But compromise goes with legislative work. Those who do not like it would do better to challenge specific compromises that benefit undeserving interests than to damn the habit of accommodation which is essential to legislative work.

C.   MAKING A CONSENSUS

§ 10–1.   Battle of the bills.   Legislative action requires a majority vote. A legislative majority may favor response to a problem, but those who want action may disagree on what action is appropriate. If everyone holds to his own conviction, the majority consensus necessary to approve legislation is not achieved. Everyone agrees the cat must be skinned, but as the argument rages over where to start skinning, the cat escapes. The legislative tactician opposing action should be at work in this situation reinforcing fears that each option (each separate, competing bill) carries destructive secondary consequences. The advocate of action, on the other hand, must work out compromises among those supporting action so that one bill ultimately receives majority support.

Contributing to the battle of the bills is bicameralism. When the two houses give separate consideration to a complicated issue, conflicting approaches to it are nearly inevitable. To minimize the problem, legislative advocates must relay messages between sponsors in the separate houses promptly as each modification occurs, asking for quick amendments to conform to the action of the other house. Amendments are more easily placed on a bill early in consideration, before attitudes become firm. If differences between the houses finally push the bill into a conference committee, the fewer the differences, the easier they are to resolve.

Another cause of conflict when several bills address a problem is pride of authorship. The pride may be assembly versus senate or it may arise from legislators or political parties vying for political credit.

§ 10–2. Irresistible title. Occasionally there develops a powerful consensus for legislative action because someone attaches an irresistible title to a proposal. The battle of the bills may slow agreement on precisely what to do, but the pressure to pass something may be overwhelming. For example, effective public relations efforts have made campaign regulation, no-fault insurance, probate reform, and environmental rights irresistible titles in various jurisdictions in recent years.

Strategically, an irresistible title situation is volatile, even dangerous. As the bill is process-ed, there may be intense efforts to add amend-ments, for this bill can carry extra baggage with-out faltering. Legislative opportunists try to hitch onto the bill secondary propositions which could not carry by themselves. Opponents of the bill, faced with the near certainty of its passage, have available only the tactics of weakening and sabotaging by amendment. Sponsors lose the check they normally have on friends of the bill, since there is little hazard of overreaching and thus killing the whole package. The normal re-straint on those who want to make it the perfect (that is, the most extreme) bill is absent. The sponsors may themselves exploit to the fullest the unusual situation in which compromise and mod-eration are not legislative necessities. A legisla-ture, in other words, occasionally finds itself on a runaway horse with a bill it must pass.

§ 10–3. **Passionate minorities.** Passionate mi-norities often have more political impact than a passive majority. Political and legislative strengths reflect the depth as well as the breadth of support for a position. In elections, the pas-sionate minority is represented most dramatically by one-issue constituencies which measure candidates by single positions, by one legislative vote out of hundreds cast. The general character of an incumbent's service or a challenger's potential is ignored, and the candidate is evaluated on whether he says the right thing about one proposition. An unfortunate by-product is the impact on other issues. Conscientious and skilled legislative work earns little political appreciation in normal circumstances, but when the electorate includes significant numbers of one-issue voters, the reward for good legislating over the whole spectrum of legislative responsibility is even less.

§ 10–4. Prepackaged compromise. One way for a legislative institution to deal with a passionate minority is through prepackaged compromise. Leaders representing the broader interests of the community negotiate with leaders of the insistent group to achieve some compromise which will protect the legislative institution from a destructive battle on the issue. Compromise serves everyone's interests. The passionate minority avoids overreaching and political backlash. If it successfully commands a majority vote in the legislature by the pressure of commitment to one issue, its legislator allies may face trouble in succeeding elections from those holding the majority opinion. On the other hand the non-passionate majority must take account of the legislative strengths of vigorous minorities (like organized

[*64*]

veterans). The best course is to work for a balanced policy response, rather than one which is
destructive, unfair, and offensive to many citizens. The benefit to the legislature and its members of having difficult, emotional issues compromised and worked out before voting is obvious.

Prepackaged compromises occur also on issues
so complex that negotiation of the final product
is best left to the interests directly involved.
Those on opposite sides of the issue often have
a continuing relationship which will outlast legislative strength at a particular time. That
strength is an unnecessarily fickle determinant
of the law and may put too high an economic
price on political victory. By accommodation the
sides may smooth out the peaks and valleys of
their relative political strength. An example is
the role of organized employers and organized
labor in helping legislative bodies work out acceptable unemployment and workmen's compensation benefits. On issues like these the interests
concerned are so politically powerful that the
final bill must exhibit a sensitive balance. Then
neither side views the law with such dissatisfaction that it bitterly throws its full force into the
next election.

When an acceptable consensus is achieved, the
legislature processes the bill with the understanding that members will not untie the package by

[*65*]

supporting a disruptive amendment, no matter how attractive the amendment appears at the moment.

D. OTHER TACTICS AND SOME REALITIES

§ 11–1. **Delayed impact debate.** During a legislative session the pace and pressure limit thoughtful reflection. Committee discussions and presentations by lobbyists compete for the attention of the legislator with other issues, with political concerns, and with personal responsibilities. The legislator takes office with the comfortable biases that carried him successfully through his election campaign. Neither a legislator's mind nor his position is easily changed.

Debate and lobbying have impact, however. Often the case made during consideration of a bill takes root and emerges as a new attitude and a new position months later when the issue arises again. Legislative advocacy is education. In legislative learning, as elsewhere, ideas often must be presented several times before they are grasped. The good legislative advocate needs a combination of patience and impatience. Patience keeps him at the task of persuading the slow-learning institution and its slow-learning members. Impatience prevents him from allowing time to run without fighting to speed along the change he desires. The advocate who is convinced he is correct can keep his morale up by presuming eventual victory while battling for quick success.

§ 11–2. **Leaning on the door.** Some legislative advocates make an opponent feel like a watchman at a door against which the relentless advocate continually leans. The opponent knows that if he ever stops pushing back, the door-leaner will move through. Few legislative experiences are more disheartening than to be caught in an unending pushing match. A quick test on the merits leaves the participant free to move on to other issues, but a test of brute endurance does not. Within legislative institutions a reputation as a door-leaner is invaluable. If the advocate seldom abandons a cause, opponents are tempted to give in with the attitude of "Eventually, why not now?" For example, the leaner may want a public institution constructed. He has a constituency behind him and is rewarded for his continual effort whether he prevails or not. The guardian of the public treasury—the no-sayer—may not receive similar appreciation from a constituency; he may even lose in popularity. Victory finally goes to the person or group with the greater endurance.

§ 11–3. **Exhausted political points.** Public cynicism about the legislature often develops from news reports of special interest victories in legislative battles. Power plays a role in legislative institutions, but a slightly longer perspective would erase much of the cynicism. Power wielders usually buy only time. Even the weakest legislators can free themselves from political and other obligations in a reasonably short period. They can then vote the merits when the issue next arises. The power-brokering lobbyist cannot complain convincingly about a vote on the merits when the legislator says: "I voted your way last time because you asked me to, but this time I see it the other way."

Press reports of legislative activities do not communicate to citizens this longer view because, when the power-broker is about to lose, he first pushes for a moderating amendment or two, then he abandons the battle so completely that the bill passes overwhelmingly. The power-broker avoids the appearance of defeat, and the bill loses the character of a great public victory over a vested interest.

The legislative advocate with a meritorious case must force the opposition to use its IOU's as soon as possible. That leaves the institution free to look to the merits, because political obligations have been disposed of. Then the advocate previously blocked by entrenched interests can pursue the strategy of leaning against the door, secure in the knowledge his cause will prevail.

§ 11–4. A dependable friend. Soon after a person takes his place as a member of a legislative body, observers spot patterns in the votes he casts. He may demonstrate consistent allegiance to party, to farm bloc, to management, to labor, to the chief executive, to public opinion polls, or to his local courthouse crowd, editor, or industry. The sophisticated legislative advocate learns whom he can depend on for support and who will likely be in opposition. He starts each lobbying effort with a quick visit to his sure friends, works his way through the likely supporters, and, finally, gets to those whose position he cannot predict. His presentation becomes more refined and effective with practice. This is a reason for starting with easy votes first. Another reason is to better gauge what compromises may be necessary. If the advocate has difficulty with his dependable friends, he will not have the votes of those legislators of more questioning attitude. With this knowledge he can trim his proposal to acceptable size early in the process, before opposition lines have hardened.

For the legislator, being thought of as a dependable friend creates problems. When he casts a vote against his political allies, they feel double-crossed and resentful, or at least let down. A respected political slogan is, "You dance with them what brung you." A legislator votes against his traditional allies with reluctance because he pays a price for doing so. The problem of being no one's dependable friend must also be understood. If the performance of a legislator is so unpredictable that he earns the trust of no constituency, he seeks re-election without a strong base of support. It is a problem to be a maverick in an institution and in a profession where loyalty is a highly valued quality.

§ 11–5. To oppose or ignore. Proponents of legislation must attract attention for the proposal. If legislators know of the proposal, they become sensitive to the problem it addresses. By communicating opposition, opponents alert legislators to the fact that the bill will have an impact, that in real life some things will be affected by its passage. If opponents ask that attention be paid to the bill, they are likely to be accommodated. Since attention is exactly what proponents of the bill need, the opposition aids significantly in starting the bill down the path toward passage. One alternative available to the legislative tactician faced with an objectionable bill is to ignore it, hoping it will die quietly. But this is a dangerous course. Proponents may quickly and privately present the case for the bill. The case may sound sensible in the absence of opposition arguments and create support for prompt action. Once a bill begins to move in a legislative institution, opposition may be too late. The dilemma is obvious.

Should the opponent step forward and pay the price of drawing attention to the proposal; or should he treat the bill as unworthy of legislative attention and run the risk of quick legislative action based on a one-sided story?

The legislative advocate may be able to cope with this dilemma by dealing directly with the agenda setters of the legislature. Discussion with the committee chairmen or staff to explain the basis for opposition and to declare readiness to marshal opposition if the bill begins to move may eliminate the hazard of quick, affirmative action. The opponent may also contact the sponsors of the bill. He can explain to them the reason for opposition, request accommodation, and communicate that there will be a fight ahead. Since the proponents obviously already know of the bill, this tactic does not draw additional attention to the proposal.

§ 11–6. Hairy arm. A bill is sometimes introduced with some obnoxious feature. Critics pounce on that frightening hairy arm as the point of vulnerability in the proposal. Sponsors may defend the provision for a time, but before the critical vote they delete the provision. Opponents are left fighting the rest of the bill, which they may not have criticized or even studied. Inclusion of the provision may have been tactical from the beginning; deleting the hairy arm gives the appearance of a compromise and an accommodation of the bill's critics. Passage of the Minnesota criminal code provides an example of the technique at work. The code as introduced made significant changes in both procedural and substantive criminal law, including provisions relating to sexual behavior. The changes relating to adultery and fornication brought vigorous attacks on the code. But when they were deleted late in the session, opponents of the code were literally left speechless. The remainder of the code passed easily.

§ 11–7. Hostage bills. Legislatures look worst when assembly and senate are locked in bitter power struggles. Since the work of the two houses is so separate, some of the moderating influences of shared conviviality and apportioned responsibility are missing when feelings run high between the houses. Also, the tool of compromise is not used daily between the houses as it is within each. Finally, dispute often arises as to whether a bill will be passed, rather than what will be in it when it does. If the dispute is over contents, the conference committee is available to work out compromise. But no established mechanism of compromise is present when the assembly enthusiastically passes a significant measure and watches its bill disappear in the files of some senate committee.

The response to this situation is often to take hostage a bill which the senate or key senators want enacted. The message is sent that the senate will get its bill passed when the bill desired by the assembly is passed by the senate. Suddenly issues are mixed, the machinery for compromise is unofficial and unstructured, the game is brinkmanship and bluff. Even in this most undisciplined of legislative situations, however, the principals usually turn in the end to the merits and to accommodation. Each house lets go of its hostage bill or bills, the session work is wrapped up, and everyone returns home with a forgiving heart—most of the time.

E. APPROPRIATIONS ADVOCACY

§ 12–1. **Procedure.** The great legislative task of giving and withholding funds for agencies, programs, and private petitioners is carried out by procedures which parallel other legislative work. The final decisions are incorporated into legislative appropriation acts. An act may cover a single item or a multitude. If it contains many items, the measure is called an omnibus appropriation bill. The omnibus bill covers some area of government activity, for example, education. It comes out of the appropriations subcommittee which holds decision-making responsibility in that field.

The legal requirements to pass an appropriation act match those of ordinary bills: three readings, majority vote, adequate title, and so on. A common departure from the ordinary bill-passing procedure is that the appropriation bill is put together and introduced *after* committee hearings and preliminary decisions on each item. What items will be in the bill and the dollar figures attached to each are determined in mark-up or allocation sessions of the committee, using the budget proposals of the executive rather than a bill to focus attention on relevant questions.

Another departure from regular bill-passing procedure arises when constitutional provisions give the executive the power to veto individual items in appropriation bills. Item veto has less impact than might be expected, however, because each item usually is itself a package of money for several programs. The executive is trapped by the packaging, which puts into most items some veto-proof element.

A distinction must be drawn between authorization of expenditures and appropriations. Legislation that establishes a new agency or program either expressly or by implication authorizes the use of public money. Funding is usually postponed for inclusion in an omnibus appropriation bill, however. This protects the prerogatives of the appropriation committee by keeping money decisions in its hands and away from committees processing bills which authorize programs. A perspective on the power of appropriation committees can be gained with the realization that authorization of a program occurs but once. On the other hand, setting spending levels is done annually or biannually thereafter by an appropriation committee which can end a program whenever it chooses, by withholding the money necessary for the activity.

§ 12.2 Subcommittee autonomy. Division of legislative labor pervades the appropriation process even more than it does other legislative functions. The volume of work routinely pushes decision making out of the full appropriation committee and into nearly autonomous subcommittees. Deference to subcommittee decision is a consequence of exhaustive hearings and study by subcommittees, coupled with the authority derived from the prerogatives of seniority typically represented in appropriations subcommittee membership. Hard work and experience give the subcommittee such knowledge that it is nearly impossible for other legislators to maintain a challenge to its decisions. Even if non-members could win the debate, the endless labor of the appropriation subcommittee gives it the privilege, in the eyes of most legislators, to be upheld even in its mistakes. Before any significant decision of an appropriations subcommittee or its parent committee is modified by floor amendment, the decision must be far out of step with the consensus of the house. The general rule of appropriation procedure is that the subcommittee decision will prevail through final passage.

After passing each house, an omnibus appropriation bill is sent to a conference committee where differences between the houses are compromised. The compromise is a mixture of splitting the difference in dollar amounts, trading off programs favored or opposed by each house, and considering the merits of the judgments made by the separate subcommittees. Membership on the conference committee represents the membership of the standing subcommittee which originally put together the bill adopted in each house.

The outsider desiring to affect appropriation decisions obviously should direct his lobbying to the membership of the subcommittee. Given the traditions of subcommittee autonomy, petitions directed to other legislators are generally ineffective.

§ 12–3. **The executive and appropriations.** In all jurisdictions, legislative appropriation work begins with a review of a formal budget containing detailed expenditure recommendations presented by the executive. The legislative rule of inertia works in the appropriations process not only to make the appropriations subcommittee dominant on the decisions within its area of jurisdiction, but also to give these early executive department recommendations a pervasive impact on appropriation decisions. An executive's budget recommendations do not come out of a void. They start with spending requests from the various agencies of government. These requests are built on past allocations and on an agency's perception of what it dares ask for. The agency request in effect puts a cap on its own appropriation, for neither executive nor legislature is apt to recommend more money than the agency requests. Therefore, lobbying for a new expenditure program or for additional financing for an old program must start at the agency.

Appropriation hearings typically involve a dialogue between the subcommittee and the department which will operate with the appropriation under discussion. The department witnesses seek to defend the level of expenditure recommended by the executive. Occasionally they may urge allotment of a larger amount consistent with what the agency originally requested, or some modest increase over the executive budget but under the agency's original request. To ask for this larger amount risks executive rancor, for it puts the agency at odds with a decision made by the executive who nominally is responsible for all agency policy.

The appropriations committee perceives its job as finding fat in the figures under discussion. It has little outside assistance in this search for extravagance. Without independent information, the committee is hard put to find a reason to cut back on executive recommendations. The committee has even less inclination to increase recommended expenditures. As a consequence, executive recommendations for government expenditures are very significant. Legislative committees make minor adjustments in specific items, but in the main follow executive recommendations. The executive's impact on legislation is nowhere more significant than in the field of appropriations.

§ 12–4. **Re-ordering priorities.** A legislature generally makes only minor changes in appropriation recommendations from the executive. It is also true that the executive generally recommends only small changes from past appropriations of the legislature. His budget is usually built on the budget adopted by the previous legislature. If the executive breaks from the appropriation patterns of the past to establish new spending priorities, his changes will be vigorously examined by the legislature. The most dominant influence on appropriation recommendations and decisions is what was done last time. Inertia rules both the executive and the legislature. To re-order priorities and to make spending decisions more rational is an important and difficult job and a major challenge to the institutions of government.

§ 12–5. Line-item versus program budgeting. Recognition of the need to improve executive and legislative appropriation decisions is producing experiments in governmental budget making at every level. Most government budgeting examines the items of expenditure to be made by an agency; for example, should an agency have three secretaries, two phone lines, $550 worth of travel, and a new executive swivel chair. Expenditures are grouped into categories: personnel, communications, travel, supplies, equipment. These line-item categories become the building blocks of the budget. Quite naturally the legislature examines newly proposed programs. These can stand up to examination, for they are likely to be timely responses to real problems. Agencies are delighted to help focus legislative attention on the new programs which they wish to add to their mission. They may then quietly continue past programs even though those programs might not in present circumstances be defensible. Re-examining and shrinking old programs is very difficult with line-item budgeting, but adding appropriations based on inflationary costs and increased clientele is easily justified. Under line-item budgeting, once something is started it is almost impossible to scale it down, let alone turn it off. The search for an alternative to the old line-item system has been prompted by the automatic, unrestrained growth of government budgets under that system.

Program budgeting has been developed as an alternative to line-item budgeting. In theory, it substitutes an examination of programs in place of the traditional examination of the objects of expenditure. The decision makers are asked to look at the service provided and at its cost, instead of at the number of employees, the amount of stationery, the kind of furniture, and the miles of travel. Program budgeting facilitates and stimulates a re-examination of all activities, whether the agency has carried on the program for one or one hundred years. The benefit of the agency activity is measured against its cost; weak programs supposedly will be discarded.

Experience with program budgeting has fallen short of expectations. Agencies of government find it difficult to price programs, and legislative committees find it difficult to verify the integrity of those price tags. The habit of appropriations committee members is to look for fat in government budgets. Textbook versions of program budgeting overlook this vital function and, more seriously, fail to take into account legislator habits. No good process has been designed to convert from line-item to program budgeting. The whole effort faces opposition or lukewarm support from the bureaucrats; agencies are not enthusiastic about giving budget bureaus, executives, or legislators real insight into agency operations when the *status quo* is reasonably attractive. The very information which would make program budgeting work well for legislators and the executive is least likely to be voluntarily revealed. The most questionable activities are likely to be hidden in some larger agency program. In some jurisdictions inadequate budget presentations have produced such frustration that program budgeting has been abandoned. In other jurisdictions, legislators and administrators are working out modified program budgets with sufficient line-item information to limit frustration while more workable program-budgeting procedures evolve.

A legislative advocate concerned with appropriations must understand the budget format in his jurisdiction. His interest will be a program interest. But if the format of the budget is line-item, he will be arguing, not for the program, but for additional employees. Or he may find himself urging increased travel allowance so present personnel can accomplish his program objectives. The lobbyist normally is interested in passing or killing or amending a bill. In the appropriation process, he will want to add an item, delete an item, or influence the amount of an allocation. Knowing what figures he wants changed and whether they stand for a program, for personnel, or for agency supplies is essential to his lobbying efforts.

If he knows nothing else about appropriations, a legislative advocate ought to know that the legislature in this area of its activity, just as in its other tasks, responds to petitions and information brought by outsiders. This is a legitimate arena for lobbying, but it is overlooked by many interests. Appropriation lobbying is mostly left to the bureaucrats.

§ 12–6. Riders. Appropriation bills include secondary provisions, called *riders*, to condition use of the funds. Riders are a common legislative device. Often a rider is not closely related to a bill and could not pass on its own merits. It seeks a free ride. Abuse is limited by bars on double-subject bills, a rider's threat to a bill's passage, and respect for normal legislative processes. These checks fail on spending bills, which makes them the favorite vehicle for riders. First, the substance and title of an omnibus bill are so broad that innumerable riders fit into it with no double-subject problem. Second, a most objectionable rider cannot kill a money bill. Third, legitimate spending control riders are camouflage for non-germane, overreaching riders.

PART II

MAKING A BILL

CHAPTER 4

IDEAS FOR LEGISLATION

A. SOURCES OF IDEAS AND BILLS

§ 13–1. Power of ideas. Intellectual inventions —ideas—are the raw material of the legislative institution. Without this raw material the legislative machinery would stop, for its machinery is designed to evaluate, modify, process, and implement ideas. H. G. Wells wrote, "Human history is in essence a history of ideas." More recently Dean Francis A. Allen wrote, "A sound idea has a power of its own." In the long perspective, the dominant force in legislative institutions is the force of intellect. It is important to know where legislative ideas come from and the channels by which ideas move to legislative consideration.

A major shortcoming of our society is the failure of its best minds to recognize the power of legislative institutions. This shortcoming leads to two disastrous consequences. First, great minds are rarely called upon to create the supply of ideas essential to the legislative process. Second, even when luck causes the intellectual raw material for legislative action to emerge, that material is often left to wither far from the legislature "and waste its sweetness on the [academic] air." The mundane-appearing task of turning theory into a bill draft does not get done—not because it is mundane, but because it is often beyond the learned or innate skills of the creator of new ideas. The gap between conceiving an idea and writing a legislative bill must be bridged. One response is to provide the skills of bill drafting to all lawyers so each can put ideas into a form useful to legislatures. Another response is to make the bridge building (bill drafting) a separate, but systematically pursued intellectual effort.

§ 13–2. **Borrowed and model bills.** Since the talent of legal invention like the talent of mechanical invention is a scarce commodity, the most efficient mechanism to obtain bills is plagarism. Neither patent nor copyright laws protect legislative invention. The idea which works well in one jurisdiction is useful to its neighbors—and free. Ideas are indeed borrowed. New proposals spread across the country, popping up in various legislatures in almost random fashion.

Legislatures also obtain a regular supply of significant bills from the National Conference of Commissioners on Uniform State Laws. A number of uniform acts are promulgated by the conference each year at an annual meeting. Between annual meetings acts are drafted, reviewed, and redrafted by committees of commissioners. Committees of the conference also make extensive use of staff help from law professors specializing in relevant fields. All 250 commissioners are lawyers—practitioners, judges, and professors—appointed by governors to represent the various states. Since uniform acts generally possess a scholarly quality beyond the capability of any state legislature working on its own, they have achieved wide acceptance.

The Council of State Governments, the American Law Institute, the American Bar Association, and numerous other organizations also produce model acts for legislatures. Anyone facing a problem that needs legislative solution ought to review the supply of uniform and model acts before trying to invent his own bill for an act. Even if a uniform or model act or an act from a neighboring jurisdiction is not totally applicable, it is infinitely easier to edit and revise a borrowed bill than to start a drafting job from scratch.

§ 13–3. **Organized interests.** Most lobbyists are hired by the organized interests that can be affected by legislative action. To represent the vested interests of the community as a lobbyist usually means to protect the *status quo*, to do defensive lobbying. Even a defensive lobbyist oc-

casionally seizes an opportunity for affirmative
action on behalf of his client, however. He knows
legislative power; he knows the institution; he
has technical legislative skills. So from time to
time he tries to cure a problem of his client by
passage of a bill. Most lobbyists also want to
play a positive role occasionally because an un-
marred record of opposing change weakens the
credibility of the lobbyist. Furthermore, his
client's willingness to pay good fees depends somewhat on the number of legislative issues affecting
the client's activities. When the lobbyist steps
forward with a bill, he increases that number by
one. And when a bill is passed, he delivers to
the client the tangible benefit of a helpful statute
to complement his usual service of blocking undesired legislation. The private interests which
are traditionally well represented at legislatures
generate a fair share of legislative bills through
the initiative of their executives, lawyers, or lobbyists.

§ 13–4. **Public officials.** Public office is won
by political campaigns. Successful campaigns
include promises of programs for senior citizens,
for employees, for parents, for taxpayers, for con-
sumers. Occasionally a candidate announces a
grand title for a program which, if he wins, forces
him to invent some substance for that title, for
example, war on poverty. Since public attention

[*86*]

focuses more on executive than on legislative races, political pressure squeezes more ideas out of executive than legislative candidates. Executive promises to respond to the real and imagined problems of the various constituencies in the electorate get broad distribution and must be followed by specific suggestions.

After he is elected, a chief executive in most jurisdictions faces a constitutional mandate to report to the legislature on the state of the state (or union). This message and his budget message place a post election burden on an executive to come up with more ideas. Individual legislators can hide behind platitudes but the executive is pushed to specifics. He borrows his ideas from wherever he can, so he conducts a search for ideas. The press also demands that executives make news. The press habitually gives pronouncements by executives prominent coverage. This forces the chief executive to an opinion-molding, leadership role.

The coercive power of chief executives to bring legislatures to action varies greatly. Generally, it is much exaggerated. When he strikes a responsive chord in the electorate and when he plays on that chord with skill, legislators challenge him at their peril. But if an executive speaks for an established consensus, he may in fact contribute little to legislative results. Legislators discover public consensus without governors or mayors or presidents.   In any event, executive offices are under more pressure to present legislative ideas than most other individuals or institutions—but they usually offer politically safe ideas.

§ 13–5. Bureaucrats.

The contribution of elected executives represents only part of the relationship between the executive-administrative branch and the legislative branch.   Present in the hallways and committee rooms of every legislature are public officials from subordinate units of government, spokesmen for various departments, and a multitude of lesser bureaucrats who carry to legislators information, assistance, and advocacy. The government establishment is particularly well represented because its lobbying is paid for by tax dollars.

Legislatures expect executive agencies to prepare bills and to lobby; agencies are thought of, rightly or wrongly, as representatives of the public interest against the private interests served by lobbyists from commerce and industry.   Agencies are an attractive substitute for legislative staff, for legislators are spared the burdens of staff selection, supervision, and discharge which are involved when the legislature creates staff of its own.   The private lobbyist, recognizing the lobbying power of bureaucrats, on many occasions starts his appeal for legislation in the bureaucracy and attempts to recruit it as an ally.

§ 13–6. Legislative studies. In the past, legislatures have been almost, though not completely, useless as bill creators. That may be changing. In recent years legislative staff has expanded significantly. A legislative employee is under somewhat the same bill-creating pressures as the executive; his employer expects something out of him. Since bills are what the institution works with, bills are what the staff man most profitably produces. However, if the staff pattern is that employees serve the institution generally, the pressure to turn out something useful is dissipated and the staff acts like the legislature itself—it simply responds to petitions from outside forces.

Legislatures do on occasion set out to produce a bill for an act. Specific studies are authorized when a problem is recognized, but no adequate solution is available. Major legislation often follows a course which includes a blue-ribbon legislative commission of some sort, perhaps with citizen members and independent staff from the academic world. In a handful of states the independent, creative study has been institutionalized by the formation of law revision commissions which work outside the legislature, but under its sponsorship. These commissions turn out legislative proposals in the private law area, proposals which meet problems otherwise ignored as the legislature works on public law issues like taxes, appropriations, and government structure.

§ 13–7. Legislators. Legislators, as politicians, often state their intention to solve a problem. They also claim later that they authored specific legislation. Legislative authorship almost always means fronting for the real creators of the legislation. It means simply to manage or sponsor the bill within the legislature. Political license permits legislators to pilfer the ideas of others. The victim of the theft is also the beneficiary, however. For when the stolen idea is introduced into the legislature as a bill for an act, it has made a start on the road to becoming a statute.

Legislators sometimes think up bills on their own; but it is unrealistic to expect legislators to be idea inventors. First, energy put into invention is lost from the more basic legislator job of judging proposed legislation. Second, and most significant, the inventive legislator is rare. Third, perhaps the best use of inventiveness, when it is found in a legislator, is in the creative editing essential to produce good legislative products. The one legislator in a hundred who learns to foresee unfortunate secondary consequences of a bill and to create amendments to avoid them should allocate his energy to do that. All the other work he does is to some extent a misallocation of a scarce ability.

Fourth, legislators, as politicians, face problems as initiators of legislation. They are restrained by the political hazard that lies in challenging conventional viewpoints. Legislators have little time to defend unconventional positions. Political speeches usually confirm audience biases. Charting new courses and selling innovative programs is more safely left to those outside the elected membership of legislative institutions.

§ 13–8. **Individuals.** Pace-setting legislative bills are a result of ideas and come most frequently from the thoughts of a series of individuals. The first person in the series probably just happens to get a creative thought. Whether the idea will then be caught and turned into a bill is dependent on chance—at least it has been in the past. The problem is that the same individual may not possess both the inspiration to create an idea and the skill to turn the idea into a bill. Legal education has failed to teach that it is useful, perhaps essential, to set up a division of labor for the production of bills. The theorists who conceive solutions to the problems of society receive no instruction in marketing their solutions to legislative institutions. Legislative draftsmen, in turn, are not taught to examine scholarly law journals to find the raw materials for exciting bills. Rather they produce pedestrian bills on order for legislators responding to political pressures. As they work, the draftsmen typically— and unfortunately—are not involved with the intellectual and creative elements in the community.

The consequences of this gap in the idea chain are illustrated by a recent dramatic victory over it. Professors Robert Keeton and Jeffrey O'Connell conducted an exhaustive study of auto accident compensation which led them in 1965 to recommend no-fault auto insurance; the Keeton-O'Connell recommendation was consistent with that of another study done at Columbia University thirty-three years earlier. The Columbia study was much discussed in academic circles, but the no-fault concept did not become a legislative issue until Keeton and O'Connell took one essential step; they included in their book a draft no-fault bill. The bill gave the Massachusetts legislature a grip on the proposal. In less than a year, no-fault auto insurance moved from ivory tower, through the Massachusetts general assembly, and to the edge of passage in the senate. Enactment took three more years, but if the bill draft had not been included in the Keeton-O'Connell book, the wait in Massachusetts and nationally might have been years longer.

There exists a need for the legal system to develop legislative solutions to the legal problems of society; for scholars to push their ideas beyond neatly researched articles for prestigious law reviews and into exhaustively edited legislative bills which are delivered to legislatures on silver platters; for editors and readers of legal publications to decide that legislative inventions deserve publication and study as interesting, influential, and scholarly work; for legislative staffs to survey intellectual sources for bill ideas and to draft bills to bridge the gap that occurs when scholars fail to turn theory into legislative proposals.

§ 13–9. **Bill creation as a process.** Bill creation is a complicated process subject to variations at every step. For example, recognizing the problem—the first step—may be the contribution of almost anyone. The second step, deciding that legislation may be the solution, can be the contribution of a politician, a political platform writer, a lawyer, a bureaucrat, an individual, a muckraker, a student, a scholar, or a committee of citizens examining the problem area. The third step is conceiving a realistic legislative response. One who recognizes the legislative potential to deal with a problem can also contribute the insight on how it should be done; indeed that insight may cause the first recognition that a legislative role exists. More commonly, invention of a bill is preceded only by the vague comment: "There ought to be a law." The observation can set a mind to work and the idea for a bill may follow.

When a legislative response is devised, the next step is drafting a bill. The inventor may produce a draft, or he may order the bill from a drafting specialist. If he makes his request to the professional drafter before the idea and response are thought through, he will be disappointed with the bill produced. Bill drafters do not turn out invention on order, at least not often. Of course, a near miss is sometimes good enough. An incomplete concept can carry the problem into the legislative and public arena where more attention can be given to the search for a solution. But usually a bill lacking essential insight will not earn a spot on a committee agenda; the competition for committee time is won by bills ready for passage.

This discussion of bill making is out of balance in one serious respect. It ignores the brute force approach to a legislative problem. Occasionally, a legislature makes a decision to tackle a problem and devise legislative action, even if there is no immediately apparent solution. This decision leads to a commitment to assemble resources for the effort. A mechanism is established to seek, to shape, to solicit, and to screen legislative proposals. All ideas which come out of the effort are evaluated. Promising starts are worked over to see if, with modification, they can do the job. Industry—at least the military industrial complex —has discovered that with adequate resources it can accomplish nearly anything. Focused in the same intense way, the legal-legislative machinery can also produce legal progress on order rather than on inspiration.   This kind of determination to solve a legal or social problem rarely exists, however.

B.   SEARCH FOR SANCTIONS

§ 14–1.   Means to an end.   Many times in drafting bills the moment of truth comes when the draftsman asks himself or the sponsor: "Now how do we make this all mean something in real life; how do we give it muscle?"   The drafter may have trouble finding the appropriate sanction to achieve the objective of the bill.   The multitude of devices available, both to penalize and to reward, makes selection difficult.   The choice is not limited to a single sanction;   a small arsenal can be assembled for one bill.   For example, the following pressuring devices have been included in legislation to force motorists to purchase no-fault auto insurance: criminal penalties (fine and jail), requirement to submit documentary proof of insurance for a motor vehicle before it can be licensed, requirement to identify an applicable insurance policy, exclusion from benefits of those who fail to insure, exposure of the uninsured to liability for negligence, and revocation of motor vehicle and driver licenses of uninsured motorists.   This list suggests the varied characteristics of sanctions.

Sanctions employ both steady and periodic pressures, both early and late stimulants, both positive and negative forces, both public and private enforcing agents, and both harsh and gentle mechanisms. Some of the sanctions push the citizen to semi-automatic compliance by making non-compliance procedurally difficult (those connected with vehicle licensing). Others punish violation through state action (criminal prosecution). Others use private action (the retained fault lawsuit). Private pressure to conform comes from insurance agent efforts to sell insurance and from peer pressure. Government agency enforcement comes through spot checks of cancellations and of the truthfulness of claimed insurance coverage on motor vehicle registration applications, followed by revocation of motor vehicle and driving licenses. The fact that the insurance purchase is sensible is a sanction which reinforces the other pressures.

Often, after a sanction is selected, the draftsman struggles to soften its impact. Sanctions should produce a satisfactory level of compliance, which need not be 100 percent, but should not punish unnecessarily. With no-fault legislation, for example, family members do not bear the same exclusions from benefits or exposure to tort liabilities as the person who should have bought the insurance; in some laws even the uninsured car owner is allowed to collect no-fault benefits after punitive deductions from those benefits.

This better serves the objective of compensating everyone which would be lost through an overly severe and therefore self-defeating sanction.

The cost and inconvenience of a sanction should be reduced as much as possible without serious loss of effectiveness. For example, to require the owner to include an insurance policy number on a license application costs less than to require a document from the insurance company stating that a policy is in effect. It is cheaper in time and money to the state, the motorist, and the insurance industry. Yet the difference in impact between the two is slight.

§ 14–2. **Criminal penalties.** The word sanction brings fines and jail terms to mind; yet these are less valuable as means to implement legislative policy than other devices. The judicious legislative draftsman searches for sanctions short of criminality, making prosecution a last resort. A criminal charge is harsh whether it leads to acquittal, brings a suspended sentence, or sends the offender to prison. It pushes the defendant to vigorous battle, rather than to the quick and continuing compliance desired by the legislature. Criminal prosecution is never self-enforcing, although the quality of being self-enforcing is the ultimate virtue in a sanction. A criminal sanction is also expensive to the state—in the cost of prosecution, in the cost of incarceration, and in its destructive impact on the life of the defendant.

In many circumstances the criminal sanction is recognized by prosecutor, judge and jury as overkill. When law enforcers find juries refusing to convict or are themselves uncomfortable with bringing particular charges, prosecution under that statute stops; the criminal sanction then becomes meaningless.

Non-criminal sanctions can also be so severe they self-destruct. In one state a statute provided that an illegal public employee strike automatically disqualified participants from any pay raise for a year. When a strike did occur, the statutory sanction made a settlement impossible until everyone agreed the statute would be ignored. The general lesson is to keep criminal and other penalties realistic, taking into account human nature. The get-tough penalty seldom accomplishes its objective.

When criminal sanctions are used, the legal pattern of the jurisdiction must be followed. Legislatures seek consistency and balance, so the penalty for violation of a new law must be in line with penalties for other violations and must fit the jurisdiction's standard classifications of felony, gross misdemeanor, misdemeanor, petty misdemeanor or tab charges. If a bill writer does not know the habit patterns of the legislature, he may submit his bill to the legislative bill drafting agency with the criminal sanctions left blank and ask for help from the specialists. Official draftsmen have technical knowledge and sensitivity to the attitudes of their own legislature on criminal law issues. A non-specialist may draft provisions out of tune with prevailing legislative attitudes and create negative reactions to his entire bill. Criminal sanctions should be drawn with legislative acceptability the primary concern. The penalty actually applied is so much under the control of judiciary, prosecutors, parole board, and corrections agency that what a statute authorizes is usually not important, except to put the conduct into the appropriate level of criminality.

§ 14–3. Civil fine; corporate sanctions. A civil fine is non-criminal, but it is paid to the state rather than to a private person, unlike other civil payments. The fine does not brand the offender with the status of felon or misdemeanant, which gives it significant advantages over criminal penalties. With commercial misbehavior, the civil fine provides the prosecutor and judge with a useful alternative. When the misbehavior occurs in the corporate setting, the civil fine may be levied on the corporation, for criminality is often difficult to charge to specific corporate employees who may have participated to a greater or lesser extent in the illegal activity.

Corporate misbehavior challenges the draftsman and the law enforcer in special ways. Penalties on corporations spill over on innocent employees, shareholders, and even on communities
if not appropriately limited. For example, the
power to terminate the authority of a corporation
to do business in a state is seldom useful. Can-
celling a franchise or permit can also close a
business and have widespread consequences. The
draftsman writing sanctions for commercial legislation must focus some attention on the economic
impact of the sanction and on the split corporate
personality—real people and artificial entity.

§ 14–4. **Use of agencies.** Executive-administrative agencies are used to implement much legislation. To do this, agencies use whatever tools
are provided in the specific legislation plus the
flexibility inherent in administrative law. Agencies can adjust law and sanctions to the circumstances of particular cases. This power to act on
an almost *ad hoc* basis is the great strength and
the great evil of agency enforcement. Enforcement of anti-trust law is a dramatic example of
this flexibility. Anti-trust legislation has re-
mained essentially the same for decades, but anti-
trust law as enforced has varied immensely during
that time, depending on economic conditions and
Department of Justice attitudes. The history of
anti-trust illustrates that giving agencies discre-

tionary enforcement authority produces a useful power to negotiate agreements with those regulated. The anti-trust division of the Department of Justice has often cajoled monopolizers to modify their activities. In tough cases the department has negotiated consent decrees foreclosing business activities it viewed as harmful to the market place. Consent decrees involve enforceable promises not to engage in specified trade practices, not to engage in a specific business, to avoid further acquisition, or to divest parts of a business.

Most agency negotiation is less formal. Since Congress gave it responsibility to define safety standards, the Products Safety Commission has worked extensively with manufacturers. Together they decide what is feasible. The standards this commission has set represent much effort to avoid extra cost and economic dislocations to industry, even at the price of slower implementation and reduced effectiveness. State and federal environmental protection agencies engage in the same type of bargaining with various interests to decide what should be done, when it should be done, what will be done voluntarily, what must be forced, and what alternatives are available. This negotiation is continual, so new knowledge can be put into the process and decisions adjusted accordingly. If legislatures had imposed specific rules and deadlines, appropriate adjustment to new facts would be difficult.

Of course, the captive regulatory agency is a familiar phenomenon. The failure to build into laws some degree of insurance against agency surrender to political expediency is a serious failure. Too often legislatures leave the politically tough work—laying down the law—to an agency. Almost inevitably, accommodation occurs between agency and industry. To protect against excessive compromise a legislature must provide private remedies to back up and buck up the agency. A legislature should also write the law with sufficient courage to set an example the agency cannot ignore and to limit the discretion of the agency so that it cannot sabotage the legislature's objectives.

§ 14–5. Licenses, permits, charters, and franchises. The legal system keeps control of many activities by licenses or variations such as permits, charters, and franchises granted by agencies or local governments under legislative authorization. The agency granting the license may do so on a selective basis to limit participation to qualified persons, to control the intensity of competition, to ration a scarce resource like television channels, or to maintain monopolies when competition does not make economic sense, as with telephone service. If the license is granted indiscriminately, but for a fee, the purpose may be to limit the number of participants by imposing a charge; to raise revenue; to gather information of value to the public or government, for example, building permits; or to keep a record of those in the licensed business, for example, pawnbrokers.

An inherent part of licensing is the power to revoke or temporarily suspend them. This sanction is extensively and effectively used. Driver license suspensions are obvious examples. Liquor dealer license suspensions as punishments for sales to minors, restaurant license suspensions for sanitation violations, disbarment of attorneys, and nonrenewal of radio station licenses for lack of public service are other examples.

The legal tool of licensing allows an innovative draftsman much flexibility. For example, to reduce the overpopulation of deer hunters in the woods at one time (which causes hunters to shoot one another) several states now issue part-of-season licenses. In one of these states, hunters may choose licenses either for the two opening days, for the following six days, or for the ten closing days. The later periods give more hunting days, but a depleted and more alert herd to hunt. This system keeps about two-thirds of the hunters out of the woods during each period.

§ 14–6. Publicity; education; information. Publicity is a significant, but often cruel sanction. It strikes with bare accusation, even with no proof of violation. One person with a common name or routine job may suffer little from publicity about his missteps; another person may pay severely in public and private life from a similar report. Therefore, lawmakers often try to control the time and extent of publicity, so as to put a check on its impact. Prosecuting attorneys, police, health inspectors, and other law enforcement agents receive legislative direction to keep their activities confidential. The identity of juveniles is withheld even after a judicial finding of guilt. Officials are authorized to purge criminal records when specified periods elapse.

While there are valid reasons to limit public information in the interest of justice, the draftsman searching for ways to make legislation effective is more apt to authorize or promote publicity than to restrict it. Legislative policy, supported by the dictates of press freedom, requires that prosecutions, convictions and administrative sanctions be public. Publicity can be used to prevent criminal activity by alerting potential victims. For example, when they learn that confidence game operators are active in a community, officials issue press statements describing the scheme. The operators may be scared off or, because of the publicity, enough new evidence may be brought to the agency so prosecution is possible.

Legislation sometimes requires private parties to disclose information. Forced disclosure is the main sanction for regulation of the securities marketplace, through the requirement that new stock issues be accompanied by a prospectus and that insider buying and selling be disclosed in periodic reports. For a period, television stations, under FCC pressure, ran one anti-smoking public service spot for each three or four cigarette commercials. This anti-smoking sanction had a significant impact, judging by smoking statistics, and tobacco companies negotiated with the FCC for a rule against all broadcast advertising of tobacco to end those effective public service ads. The cigarette package health warning and other label requirements like ingredient and nutrition information, safety warnings, date coding, and batch identification are examples of mandatory information disclosure used to implement legislative policy.

Rights often are conditioned on notice to others, for example, recording deeds to protect property title, prompt notice of injury to recover on workman's compensation claims, and filing financing statements to protect security interests in commercial assets.

Freedom of information acts open the activities of government itself to examination and to the sanction of publicity. Finally, legislatures appropriate significant funds so agencies may engage in public education to help citizens make better decisions in areas like nutrition, health care, agricultural practices, and tax return preparation.

§ 14–7. Private rights. To create or modify rights for private parties against others is a major sanction available to draftsmen. For example, unfair and deceptive trade practices acts give competitors who are injured rights to recover actual damages, to enjoin, and to obtain a variety of other relief.

Legislation often authorizes special remedies. The best known is treble damages, which was established as a private remedy because a liability simply to repay an unjust gain is an inadequate deterrent to continuing misconduct. It is much more effective if a plaintiff can say: "Give my money back. Three times!" It is especially effective when the victim's lawyer goes looking for others who also can get repaid three times, less the lawyer's fee. That makes the whole scheme unprofitable.

The triple recovery is based on experience, habit, tradition, and a rough sense of justice. A higher penalty might turn the victim into the exploiter; and experience shows treble damages are enough to deter. Legislators are familiar with the sanction. The bill sponsor who seeks less is asked to explain why he is so soft on the offender; the sponsor who seeks more is asked to explain why he wants to enrich careless victims and sharp-shooting lawyers. It is easier tactically to stick with the familiar remedy. In circumstances where treble damages are potentially unjust, draftsmen may include a maximum or a minimum on the recovery.

Legislation establishes many rules of law which profoundly influence private rights. For instance, the evidentiary statute which limits testimony about conversations with persons who have died makes some contracts not provable and legally worthless. Legislatures have passed guardianship statutes which throw a protective blanket over wards, relieving them of liabilities they would otherwise bear. The legislatively established right to cancel some contracts during cooling-off periods is a powerful rule of private law which controls door-to-door sales practices. Statutes of limitations, as rules of law regulating private relationships, carry out a legislative policy to end old disputes. The draftsman working on a bill must decide when disputes under the bill should terminate. Since the answer is subjective and varies from issue to issue, shaping a limitation section is one of the most difficult tasks for legislative draftsmen and other policymakers.

§ 14–8. Suggestions on sanctions. A few summary generalizations about sanctions are appropriate at this point.

(a) Multiple sanctions should be considered and used if possible. Different citizens respond to different kinds of pressures. Some forces work at one stage of a transaction or procedure, but not at another.

(b) To discover opportunities to use several kinds of sanctions, the draftsman should think through the circumstances of the various actors in the chronological order of events. This helps him imagine what would impel a participant to the desired action at each stage, to imagine what vulnerabilities to sanctions exist at different times.

(c) The draftsman should inventory the public and private agents available and trace through their circumstances in chronological order to discover points at which, with appropriate statutory direction, they may act with most efficacy to achieve the goals of the bill. Since government agencies have imperfections, private sanctions, self-help and self-actuating devices are invaluable.

(d) A bill should be examined to find ways to cushion its sanctions. The draftsman and sponsor are wise to walk in the shoes of those who will suffer the sanctions proposed. It is also necessary to think of the associates of those who offend against the legislation. Sanctions should not spill over and hurt the innocent.

(e) Enforcement should piggyback on other procedures as much as possible. If some existing machinery can achieve the goal of the legislation, new machinery should not be created.

(f) Affirmative rather than punitive means should be used to achieve legislative goals. For example, free trash collection in a community keeps yards cleaner than relentless prosecution of those who fail to keep their yards free of debris without such help.

(g) Harsh sanctions should not be equated with effectiveness. A modest penalty which is actually imposed accomplishes more than a severe penalty which is ignored.

CHAPTER 5

BILL DRAFTING

A. BILL DRAFTING TECHNIQUES

§ 15–1. **A first draft.** A bill drafting project goes nowhere until some words are put on paper. Bill drafting is hard writing, and the intimidating effect of a clean sheet of paper is great. Things move along, however, when the draftsman realizes his work will likely be rewritten several times. It moves fastest when the copying machine is used to borrow a first draft. In complicated bills many sections can be borrowed from parallel legislation. Comparable legislation also provides a check list of what must be included in the draft bill. For example, if the bill establishes a new administrative agency, a check of prior legislation setting up an agency will indicate the need to provide for method of appointment, terms, applicability of civil service rules, salaries, powers, duties, and procedures to be followed. The copying machine is also a useful tool in drafting amendatory bills, because writing in new words and crossing out old words on a copy of the statute provides a quick first draft. The draftsman who must begin without any statutory model can expect the project to take a long time.

One way to speed drafting is to view a bill as a collection of separate parts. The easiest provisions can be drafted first. As sections accumulate they are put in sequence; there is freedom to insert forgotten provisions at any time and to rearrange everything if a more logical structure comes to mind. A grand outline is unnecessary, for sections are surprisingly self-contained. The most powerful section is often the easiest to draft. It will state the rule of law to be imposed, or the mission of the agency to be created, or the newly imposed task to be performed. The detailed and difficult provisions are those that define when and where and to whom the law is applicable. They can be drafted later. Usually they grow slowly through a first rough draft to seventh and eighth versions as the draftsman's imagination suggests appropriate limitations and exclusions or expansions of coverage. Eventually, the draftsman produces a product he dares turn over to someone else for comment, or study, or further drafting—or introduction. Only the simplest or roughest bills go from the start of drafting to formal introduction with one draftsman.

The struggle for a first draft can be the work of a scholar bringing his academic insight into real world terms; it can be a bureaucrat dealing with a problem of his agency; it can be a lawyer drafting a bill responsive to his client's problem; it can be a lobbyist putting together the bill he will try to sell to the next legislative session. In any of these instances the bill should be turned over to the legislature's professional bill drafters for editing before it is introduced.

§ 15–2. **The last draft.** Every legislature has an office to perform the full range of bill drafting services. Its main responsibility is to put the final technical polish on all bills to be introduced. These offices routinely receive bills drafted by others with a request to put them in form for introduction. When a preliminary draft is provided, the office may give it substantive review and suggest helpful changes. In other cases the office simply makes the style of the bill accord with the detailed technical rules which outsiders cannot be expected to know. These offices process bills when requested to do so by a legislator, so outside interests tap this resource through the intervention of a legislator. A legislative advocate ought to use these skilled, free services to improve the quality of bills in which he has an interest.

§ 15–3. **Middle drafts; editing.** Between the first draft of a bill and the enacted statute, there may be innumerable rewrites. Some sections fall into good form quickly and easily. Other sections, usually the critical sections setting out the extent of applicability of the law, cause repeated stumbles. Each redraft stimulates new insights into the complex issues addressed. Like a musician working over a difficult passage, the draftsman will draft and redraft a single section in an effort to make it match the precision of the rest of the bill. As it moves through multiple drafts, a bill also tends to grow. Additional problems come to mind and sections are added to deal with them.

The need for new insights and new provisions during rewriting suggests the value of bringing fresh minds to the effort. One person's imagination is not adequate to put together any complex bill. The primary draftsman should pass it to others for review, comment, and drafting help. He should allow others to discover problems on their own, then alert them to specific sections he knows need additional work. An initial reading without briefing helps the new reader spot difficulties the primary draftsman has not recognized. This is of great value, for finding problems in drafts, like medical diagnosis, is essential to the cure.

Another advantage of involving others in the editing of a bill is the political benefit of giving them some pride of authorship. When a person's suggestion is added, a part of the bill belongs to him and he is likely to treat the whole bill more affectionately. Political managers of a bill may even invite potential or certain opponents to participate in editing. If opponents can be accommodated early with reasonable amendments or if they can be convinced of the sponsor's good will, their later opposition is moderated or avoided. Those adversely affected by a bill also read it with their critical faculties stimulated; they spot defects. It helps to learn of their embarrassing insights during private discussion of a proposed draft, rather than in a public hearing. Even if an opponent springs his criticism at a hearing, the sponsor can quickly turn the embarrassment around by saying: "I wish you had written me about that problem when I asked for your suggestions in October."

§ 15–4. **Horizontal editing.** A most useful drafting technique is to examine a bill repeatedly from beginning to end, each time editing out only one or two kinds of defects. For example, one examination might concentrate on the sequential numbering of the sections and subsections to correct errors which slip into a bill when provisions are eliminated, added, or rearranged. The same examination might also check cross references between sections. This technique is called horizontal editing. It recognizes that the mind cannot be alert to everything at once. Looking for a few specific defects helps uncover mistakes which might be missed during an unfocused review of the bill.

Horizontal editing works on the most complex and subtle aspects of a bill, as well as for simple grammar and style problems. Even tactical and political difficulties can be avoided by horizontal editing. For example, a bill may address a secondary problem which is insignificant compared to its main thrust. The subsidiary provision may necessitate a referral to an additional and dangerous committee. Reading the bill with a focus on legislative tactics will disclose that fact and the offending provision can be eliminated from the draft.

§ 15–5. How careful a job? Bill drafters face tight deadlines in much of their work; there is competition for their time from other bill requests and other responsibilities. In each drafting effort there comes a time to call a halt, to order up a clean draft to hand over to those who will carry the bill on to its fate. The bill drafter may have only a faint impression of what that fate will be. The request to draft the bill may come from a weak legislator whose bills are usually ignored. In that case, a quick, superficial draft seems appropriate. The idea may be significant, however, and the draftsman cannot know who might take up the issue. He also has self respect; to send out a superficial draft offends him and may hurt his professional reputation. As a consequence, most legislative drafting offices do average work on almost all bills. Bills headed for oblivion are as carefully drafted as major bills destined for legislative passage. The trivia is over-drafted; the major bills are not drafted well enough. Drafting resources should be better allocated. The drafter should know if the bill is being drafted to be passed or to start discussion; if he is not told, he should ask.

§ 15–6. Format of bills. Bills are drafted in different formats for different jurisdictions. The device used nearly everywhere when statutes are being changed is to draw bills so both the old and the new law appear in the draft. Words, phrases, sentences, and paragraphs to be removed by passage of the bill are marked by ~~interlining~~. Words, phrases, sentences, and paragraphs to be added are marked by <u>underlining</u>. This system permits an easy comparison of present and future law. The change can be evaluated with a minimum of dependence on explanation by witnesses. Major new legislation usually involves amendment and repeal of old law and enactment of new provisions.

The legislative advocate can rely on the drafting office to do the behind-the-scenes detail work. The time pressures on the drafting office become intense, however, and the closer an advocate brings his work to technical adequacy, the better relationship he will have with that helpful agency. Official bill drafting agencies prepare staff manuals on drafting which explain format and other technical details. Borrowing one of these manuals to study or buying one for regular review is a good investment of time and money. The knowledge-able advocate can take over a share of the agency labor on his project, if doing so is necessary to beat the clock at the end of a legislative session or before an important committee hearing.

B. MANDATORY PROVISIONS

§ 16–1. Title. Most state constitutions require that the subject or object of a bill be stated in its title. In these jurisdictions, a bill without a title is incomplete and invalid. In all other juris-dictions, because of legislative rules and custom, it is routine to include a title. Titles alert legisla-tors, lobbyists, press, and citizens to subjects being considered by the legislature. Titles also identify existing legislation which the bill will repeal or amend. Lobbyists carefully check the statute numbers in bill titles to spot assaults on legisla-tive law which they are hired to protect.

Titles may be written first—as a theme for the drafter—but the title must then be rewritten when the full content of the bill is known and when all references to existing law can be included. The title must be carefully drawn, for a mislead-ing or incomplete title can make an act or parts of an act invalid. Since a title is read by more people than any other part of a bill, its political impact should be carefully considered. The title must be honest, yet put the bill in a favorable light. It should not raise any suspicions or fears not justified by the real effect of the bill.

§ 16–2. Enacting clause. All bills include a formal statement like: "Be it Enacted by the Legislature of the Commonwealth of Pennsylvania." The enacting clause is constitutionally mandated in many states. It is unlikely to be omitted with modern copying equipment, although in earlier decades typists and scribes occasionally forgot the critical line. In some jurisdictions the error made the bill invalid. To give this legal effect to a mechanical error is barely defensible. The enacting clause requirement is the basis for one unusual legislative tactic. Some legislatures permit a foe to move to strike the enacting clause from a bill. If the motion carries, the bill is killed.

§ 16–3. Effective date and time. When the legislature changes the law, that change must take effect at a specific moment in time. That moment is determined by a provision in the act or by general rules applicable to all legislation in the jurisdiction. Most legislatures have adopted a provision on effective dates as part of a general act on statutory construction. The most common rule is that a bill is effective the day following adoption unless the bill specifies otherwise. Appropriation bills take effect at the start of the next fiscal year. In a few states the general rule is that bills take effect on one specific date (some weeks after the end of the session) unless the bill provides otherwise. If an effective date is included in a bill, it should be expressed as a specific calendar date. If expressed as a time interval after adoption, readers must find out when the executive signed the bill (an inconvenience) and then calculate the day it takes effect.

The obligation of the legislative advocate, staff man, or legislator is to provide a sensible effective date by asking this set of questions on each bill he examines: Can the bill be effective at once or is lead time necessary for public education or for preparatory work by agencies or others? How much lead time is necessary? Should different parts of the bill become effective at different times?

The time of day a law takes effect is also significant. A nearly insoluble problem arises if a bill is made effective at the moment of signing. Both the time of events affected by the act (for example, making a contract) and the time the act was signed may be hard to pinpoint. Many statutory construction acts make laws effective at 12:01 a. m. It is presumed that all events on an effective date occur after that hour.

§ 16–4.   Amendment and repeal sections; implied amendment and repeal.   To the extent that one act is inconsistent with another, the latter act prevails.   This allows legislatures and draftsmen to amend and repeal by implication;   that is, they may gloss over past legislation and impose a new rule, yet leave the old, dead law on the statute books.   Lawyers and other citizens may then be surprised to find that an apparently relevant act has been superseded.   This negligent legislating leaves statute books in semi-chaos, full of inconsistencies which can only be sorted out by finding the date of each enactment and giving effect to the words last adopted.   Various amendatory laws may have to be examined in detail to discover when the inconsistency came into the law.

Another rule of statutory interpretation provides that apparently inconsistent provisions are given effect if they can be reconciled in any way.   Implied repeal is not favored;   courts try to find some way to give effect to any provision of statute which has not been repealed.   The practice is justified because a legislature can easily strike from the law any provision it wants to terminate.   In theory, the rule pushes legislatures to carefully clean out obsolete sections of statutes.   In reality, legislators are unaware of this subtle rule of interpretation.   A jurisdiction's law would be much improved if legislators, staff, and lobbyists were conscious of the need to keep statutes clean and consistent.

It is difficult to draft bills which repeal or amend all inconsistent statutes. First, the inconsistencies must be found; then decisions must be made whether to repeal or rewrite. Often an inconsistent provision cannot be repealed, either because parts must continue in effect or because circumstances not covered by the new law must remain under the old. The draftsman must define the boundary lines of applicability between the old and new rules—a hard task. The task usually arises when the new bill is nearly complete and the draftsman is eager to get on to his next project. Too often he takes the easy road and relies on repeal by implication to dispose of the inconsistent provisions.

One middle road is available. When a semi-inconsistent provision turns up, the draftsman can decide whether the old or the new law should have priority. Then he can insert the following useful phrases: "notwithstanding the provision of" and "subject to the provisions of." The effect is to alert anyone who finds either section to the presence of the other section and to indicate which is to be applied when they overlap.

Of no use—prima facie proof of incomplete work in fact—is the phrase: "other law to the contrary notwithstanding." The rule making the last act effective in cases of inconsistency does the same thing as this phrase, so it is redundant at best.   If the draftsman knows or thinks contrary law exists, he should find it and repeal or amend it.

C.   TECHNICAL PROVISIONS

§ 17–1.   Statutory construction act.   All legislative drafting is done upon a base of legal rules relevant to legislation.   These rules are incorporated into each act adopted by a legislature. Most states have codified the rules into a statutory construction act.   Included are canons of statutory interpretation, effective date provisions, definitions for standard terms, miscellaneous directions to bill drafting agencies, and a variety of other provisions.   Every lawyer and anyone working with a legislature should become familiar with this part of the statutory law.   Some of the provisions are stunning on first reading because they are so basic, like the provision: "Words of one gender include the other genders."   This sentence is law in at least 45 states.   It also is section 4 of the Uniform Statutory Construction Act.   Particularly useful provisions of that act, which parallel legislation in effect in many jurisdictions, are:

Section 3.   The singular includes the plural, and the plural includes the singular.

Section 4. Words of one gender include the other genders.

Section 5. Words in the present tense include the future.

Section 6. The word "week" means 7 consecutive days.

Section 8.

> (a) In computing a period of days, the first day is excluded and the last day is included.
>
> (b) If the last day of any period is a Saturday, Sunday or legal holiday, the period is extended to include the next day which is not a Saturday, Sunday or legal holiday.
>
> (c) If a number of months is to be computed by counting the months from a particular day, the period ends on the same numerical day in the concluding month as the day of the month from which the computation is begun, unless there are not that many days in the concluding month, in which case the period ends on the last day of that month.

Section 11. A quorum of a public body is a majority of the number of members fixed by statute.

Section 24. The repeal of a repealing statute does not revive the statute originally repealed or impair the effect of any saving clause therein.

§ 17–2. Non-retroactivity and savings clauses.

The Uniform Statutory Construction Act contains two provisions dealing with the problem of retroactivity.

Section 14, a non-retroactivity clause, reads:

(a) A statute is presumed to be prospective in its operation unless expressly made retrospective.

Section 25, a savings clause, reads:

(a) The reenactment, revision, amendment, or repeal of a statute does not except as provided in subsection (b):

> (1) affect the prior operation of the statute or any prior action taken thereunder;

> (2) affect any validation, cure, right, privilege, obligation, or liability previously acquired, accrued, accorded, or incurred thereunder;

> (3) affect any violation thereof or penalty, forfeiture, or punishment incurred in respect thereto, prior to the amendment or repeal; or

> (4) affect any investigation, proceeding, or remedy in respect of any privilege,

obligation, liability, penalty, forfeiture, or punishment; and the investigation, proceeding, or remedy may be instituted, continued, or enforced, and the penalty, forfeiture, or punishment imposed, as if the statute had not been repealed or amended.

(b) If the penalty, forfeiture, or punishment for any offense is reduced by a reenactment, revision, or amendment of a statute, the penalty, forfeiture, or punishment (if not already imposed) shall be imposed according to the statute as amended.

In the several dozen states which have provisions like Section 25, saving clauses in individual acts are unnecessary.

Common law bars retroactive effect in most cases and canons of construction presume an intent of non-retroactivity with or without statutory affirmation. The statute simply codifies common law. Although having two sections implies some difference between non-retroactivity and savings clauses, they are two sides of a single coin. One covers additions to statutory provisions; the other covers repeals or subtractions from the statutes. But both do the same thing; that is, they apply old rules to the past and new rules to the future. It does not make any difference whether the change occurs from striking out words, adding words, or substituting words.

§ 17–3. Severability clauses. Legislatures at one time faced a judicial attitude that if any part of a legislative act was invalid the presumed intent of the legislature was that the entire act should fail. This rule caused legislatures first to include severability clauses in most acts and later to include general severability rules in statutory construction acts. The uniform act contains the following typical provision:

> Section 16. If any provision of a statute or the application thereof to any person or circumstance is held invalid, the invalidity does not affect other provisions or applications of the Act which can be given effect without the invalid provision or application, and to this end the provisions of the statute are severable.

This provision makes severability clauses in individual acts unnecessary. Courts interpret severability clauses to accord with the basic rule of statutory interpretation, that the intent of the legislature controls. Severability saves that which the court believes the legislature wants saved, but no more. Courts did much the same with the old presumption against severability; they permitted litigants to argue that the legislature intended to keep in effect those portions of an act not interwoven with invalid provisions. History shows severability clauses only change the initial presumption and shift the burden of persuasion as to what parts of an act can stand alone. Shifting that burden makes severability sections worthwhile, but it seldom changes the outcome of a case.

§ 17–4. Purpose clause. Opinion is divided on whether introductory purpose sections improve or harm legislation. They are defended on the basis that an opening section stating a bill's objective helps a first-time reader understand a bill. However, the bill itself must be studied to evaluate what its working sections really do. Purpose clauses are also defended on the ground that they aid in statutory interpretation. To a court looking for legislative intent, a purpose clause may seem useful. But opponents and proponents of a piece of legislation insert qualifications and limitations in its working provisions, not in its purpose clause. To decide tough questions of meaning, courts must follow the substantive provisions of a law and the requirements of justice in the case before them, rather than nonfunctional purpose clauses.

One compromise available is to include a purpose section in a bill to gain the political advantage of its explanation and its public relations message. Then, when the bill moves close to final passage, the purpose section can be stricken as unnecessary. This keeps the statute books shorter and deprives courts of purpose-section sermonettes to use as crutches when they interpret the law. After a bill is passed, most purpose clauses are seldom read anyway.

§ 17–5. **Short title.** The mandatory title on a bill is dropped when the act is placed in a statutory compilation. Legislation thus loses this helpful description. When a bill establishes a separate program or set of rules, an identifying name included as section 1 is useful, like: "This act may be cited as the Crime Victims Reparation Act." The short title, which follows the enacting clause, is adopted along with the substantive rules of the act. Statute indexes usually include a list of short titles or popular names of acts; these provide a quick way to locate the statute.

Short titles have political value; a name gives a proposal a bit of personality and individuality. It also gives a bill a handy identifier which helps in the legislative process and with headline writers. Usually a short title is appended only to a bill of real substance, however. If a draftsman puts one in a trivial bill, it may bring ridicule to the measure and harm its prospects.

§ 17–6. **Headnotes.** Headnotes are the bold-face captions on individual sections which flag the substance of each separate section. They should not be confused with the short titles which apply to a series of sections and are part of the act. The law in each jurisdiction determines whether headnotes are part of the law or only an editorial device. The rule will appear in the statutory construction act of the jurisdiction. Even if headnotes are not official legislative language, some acts are exceptions to the general rule. The Uniform Commercial Code, for example, was written with the headnotes as part of the law. Therefore, even if the usual rule in a jurisdiction is to ignore headnotes in statute interpretation, the UCC headnotes are part of the law and contribute to the act's meaning along with all its other words.

D.   DEFINITIONS

§ 18–1. Power and utility of definitions. A legislature may make a term in an act mean anything it wants. If an act says: "For the purposes of this act 'up' means down," then *up* does mean *down*—although that is not a helpful definition. Used properly, definitions are powerful tools to make bills shorter, more understandable, and more precise. This tool is overused, misused, and abused, however. Draftsmen have great opportunity to improve or damage a bill through definitions.

While definitions are placed at the beginning of a bill, they should be written last. Then the need for each included definition is clear. Ambiguities are discovered when a complete draft is under review. The draftsman is likely to add clarifying definitions to a bill at that time. Before adding definitions, the draftsman should try to rewrite the ambiguous provision. Modifiers and qualifying sentences can be inserted. If these additions make the section too complex, the draftsman is forced to treat the problem somewhere else in the bill. He should prefer a substantive provision which tackles the problem directly. He may say, for example, "This act does not apply to proprietary trade schools." As a last choice, he turns to definition, "The term 'college' means . . .".

Definition to achieve clarity is used when no word in the dictionary, even with the help of modifiers, expresses an idea with sufficient precision. Obviously the best natural word should be used and its statutory definition should add to or change its dictionary meaning as little as possible. Definition shortens a bill when one reasonably accurate term can be defined and substituted for a long or awkward enumeration which would otherwise be repeated several times in the bill. Defining *person* to make it cover almost all legal entities is the classic example of a definition that saves words.

§ 18–2. Avoid substantive rules. One reason to hold off writing definitions until late in drafting is to reduce the temptation to insert substantive rules into definition sections. Rules should be straightforward commands, not definitions. Draftsmen regularly misuse definitions by putting too much substantive law into them. Bills drawn in this style are confusing to read. A definition encompassing the central idea of a bill is complex. Terms used in the definition themselves need definition. The draftsman ends up with three and four definitions modifying the main definition. It is nearly impossible to edit the mess. Usually the bill can be repaired only if it is taken apart and put back together in a wholly different format. Worst of all, when the draftsman puts the heart of the bill in a definition, what he writes for the main section is secondary and has meaning only if the reader plugs in the definition.

A drafting technique which avoids the hazard of substantive rules inserted in definition sections is to use cross references between substantive sections instead of definitions. For example, a bill may use an applicability section to define those persons subject to the rule of the bill. The section laying out the rule itself then may say: "Those persons described in [the section on applicability] shall . . . ". Both sections are full of substance; and neither masquerades as definition.

§ 18–3.   Means, not includes. Definition should
tell a reader what the defined terms means. The
draftsman   should   say: "College   means
.   .   .". If his definition does not cover everything he wants in the definition, his use of *means*
is misleading.   He should rewrite the definition
or not define the term. When the purpose of the
definition is to add some marginal ideas to the
natural meaning of the term, the draftsman can
say "College includes   .   .   ." If the intent is
to take marginal things out, the draftsman can
say: "College does not include   .   .   ." *Includes* and *does not include* appropriately replace
means in definitions if the purpose is to rely primarily on the natural meaning of the term while
sharpening the edges.   Still, nine times out of
ten, definitions should be written with the verb
means—and the draftsman should write the definition tightly enough so it says what he intends.

§ 18–4.   Other rules about definitions. While
the main rule on definitions is that they should
not include substantive provisions, there are other important rules:

(a) Natural meanings. Defined terms should
have natural meanings. Readers are careless
about checking back to definitions, so any unnatural meaning is missed by a significant number.
Unnatural meanings are unnecessary. The Eng-

lish language has words which alone or in combination come close to almost any intended meaning.

(b) Bound by definition. Once a term is defined, the draftsman must stay with that definition. Whatever the context, the defined term carries its statutory definition rather than Webster's. One routine item for horizontal bill editing is to find each sentence in which a defined term is used and read the definition into it. If the definition does not fit the sentence, a different word must be substituted.

(c) Juxtapose definitions. If a defined term is used only once or twice in a bill, its definition should be relocated in the section where the term is used or eliminated and the idea incorporated into the text. The definition should not be hidden at the beginning of a bill if it can be placed where the reader will more likely see it when he needs it.

(d) Keep to a minimum. Unnecessary definitions should not be used. A reader expects each definition to change the normal meaning of the defined term in some way. If it does not do that, the definition adds confusion to the bill, not clarity. Since definitions modify the natural meaning of terms, a defined term is dangerous to a reader who overlooks the definition.

E. COMMON DRAFTING ERRORS

§ 19–1. Horizontal editing again. Drafting errors cannot be avoided in initial drafting; they must be found and corrected with editing. Adequate bills on complex subjects are produced only through repeated review of the bill, each time focusing on one or two kinds of likely problems. Each bill should also be passed from one draftsman to another for review. The initial draftsman, even if he edits his work expertly to eliminate errors, overlooks some defects. A competent draftsman reading someone else's bill usually discovers mistakes. An error spotted by the second draftsman is often one of several of the same type; each mistake therefore is a guide to productive horizontal editing.

A further reason to search for defective writing in bills is that drafting errors are symptoms of policy weakness. Draftsmen make grammatical errors when they lack a focus on underlying policy. For example, if the verb is singular and the subject is plural, the draftsman probably had no firm focus on who or what the subject should be.

§ 19–2. Shall and may. *Shall* is the most powerful word in the draftsman's inventory. It must not be squandered by misuse. *Shall* must not be wasted by being used to put verbs in the future

tense. The future tense is seldom needed in statutes, for a legislative act applies to the ever-
present present. The novice draftsman finds it
unnatural to write in the present tense, since he
is thinking about the future. Once he learns to
think in terms of the time when the statute is
read, the present tense comes easily. Then those
invaluable *shalls* are saved for their proper use.

The proper use of *shall* is to give an order.
Shall is a word of command. If legislative intent
is to give permission, *may* is used. Between command and permission there is a middle ground—
direction. In everyday speech the auxiliary verb
should is used to give direction; for example,
"You should file two copies." Statute style bars
should, however. Statute style also bars *must*
as the imperative verb. Eventually these style
rules may be modified, but for the foreseeable future draftsmen are left with *shall* for both command and direction. The draftsman, therefore, is
forced to use context to separate orders from
directions.

Editing bills for *shall* and *may* and *must* and
should produces more corrections of substance
than any other single horizontal editing effort.
The change of a *shall* to a *may* is of obvious significance. Defensive lobbyists attack the *shalls*
in bills to protect their clients from legislative intrusion. The skilled draftsman follows the lead
of these knowledgeable professionals. He focuses

on each *shall* and each *may* to see if the bill
needs a muscular *shall* inserted in a key place or
if the bill antagonizes with an offensively com-
manding *shall* where a *may* would suffice.

Horizontal editing to correct one other bill
weakness can conveniently be combined with a
review of auxiliary verbs. Often when a sentence
must express a negative, the negative is inserted
in the subject by one small word at the beginning
of the sentence: *"No* draftsman shall . . ."*.
It is clearer to insert the negative in the verb
phrase immediately after *shall* or *may* and just
before the rest of the verb; for example, "A
draftsman shall *not* hide the negative."

§ 19–3. Or, and, and/or. *And* is conjunctive;
or is disjunctive; *and/or* is not used in legislation
by draftsmen who have self-respect, training, and
iron wills. *And* can be both conjunctive and disjunctive, so *and/or* is unneeded. If ambiguity
persists, the context must be adjusted or some
phrase used to make clear that "any or all" or
"one or more" is the intended meaning.

The difference between *and* and *or* is often of
serious substantive consequence. Perhaps because the words are so small, their significance is
often missed until horizontal editing focuses attention on the impact if *and* is used when *or* fits.
One example can make the point: "To qualify, a
person shall be an owner of valid record title *and*

(*or?*) be in possession of the property." Which word is right? Either makes legal and grammatical sense, so the choice depends on the purpose of the legislation.

§ 19–4. Misplaced duty. Statutes are bossy; they give orders. Draftsmen regularly forget to direct the orders to someone. For example: "School buildings shall have fire alarms." It is difficult to hold a building accountable for its failure to have an alarm system, but this provision places the duty on the building. The problem is not simply one of style; to determine who has responsibility is often difficult. In this example, the school board, the school superintendent, the local fire department, the state fire marshall, the school architect, the electrical contractor, or the general contractor might be responsible. Until the writer of a bill focuses on who must carry out the legislative purpose, he has skipped a key part of law writing. To work, the law must give orders to and impose sanctions on some human. For example: "School superintendents shall provide for installation and maintenance of fire alarms in all school buildings."

§ 19–5. Jargon. A mental quirk of many bill writers compels them to fill their bills with *such*. Such usage offends readers not brainwashed to think such words belong in such writing. A good draftsman takes out almost every *such*. He will delete some; he will substitute *the, this,* or *these* for others; he will insert honest words which contribute legal meaning in place of still others. To use *such* is unnecessary and bad bill drafting.

Professor Reed Dickerson in *Legislative Drafting* (an excellent, short and useful book) lists additional forbidden words:

above (as an adjective)	said (as a substitute for "the," "that," or "those")
aforesaid	
afore-mentioned	same (as a substitute for "it," "he," "him," etc.)
and/or	
before-mentioned	
herein	to wit
hereinafter	whatsoever
hereinbefore	whensoever
provided that	wheresoever

Professor Dickerson did not exhaust the available examples of bill drafting jargon. To present even this short list may do as much harm as good. It would be better if bill writers were not exposed to the words in the first place.

To eliminate jargon, an editor looks for style, words, and phrases which say in stilted ways what should be said simply, which say indirectly what should be said directly, which say with technical words what should be said with everyday vocabulary. The bill writer who uses legalistic words wants to make his bill sound legal. But he loses the virtue he should most desire—clear meaning. A good draftsman aims at a style of writing worthy of his brightest, non-lawyer acquaintance.

§ 19–6. Grammar. Good legislative drafting, which varies little from other good writing, requires the draftsman to adhere to the basic rules of grammar. Consistency in expression cannot be sacrificed to achieve a more interesting style, however. Synonyms cannot be inserted for variety, because different words are presumed to convey different meanings. For example, if *bank* and *banking facility* are both used in an act, the reader appropriately expects a different meaning for each term. For one meaning, only one term should be used.

A great grammatical challenge in bill drafting is to maintain parallelism (consistent style) throughout a list of items or ideas. The solution is to develop consistency in thought, for grammatical breakdowns occur when items in a list are thought of in different ways. For example, a list of duties falls apart grammatically if the duties are not imposed on the same person, if some are conditional and others are absolute, if some are active and others are passive, if some are procedural and others are substantive, if some are affirmative and others are negative. The draftsman who finds a mixed-up list in a bill almost invariably improves the substance of the bill when he puts the list into a consistent grammatical form.

Basic grammatical style rules applicable to statutes are: use the present tense, use the indicative or imperative mood rather than the subjective, use the active voice rather than the passive, use the singular in preference to the plural, and use the third person.

A final grammatical direction is to make the antecedent of every pronoun unmistakable; edit every bill horizontally once matching pronouns and antecedents.

F. TACTICAL DRAFTING

§ 20–1. Involve opponents. One tactic helpful in getting a bill passed is to bring opponents into the drafting process so deeply that they voice all their questions, objections, twits and rages while the bill is being written and prior to the time the legislative committee gathers to consider the bill. An invitation to participate in drafting disarms opponents. It can hardly be refused, for a refusal shows an intransigence not in accord with the compromising spirit of legislative institutions. Nearly every significant bill is eventually co-written by supporters and those who originally wanted it to disappear like the cheshire cat. Starting early to listen, to bargain, and to accommodate is sound strategy. This strategy is harder to implement than to state. A semi-official or official arena for meeting is usually needed. An executive-administrative agency invitation to participate is especially difficult to ignore. Preliminary bill drafts for discussion are necessary. Bill drafts focus discussion on the precise solution offered and on the alternatives available for each provision. They prevent diversionary and pointless arguments over principles and get the participants working at actual words and concrete ideas. Discussion drafts come from almost anywhere—the ivory tower, the agency, an interest group, a citizens' lobby, an individual, the legislative staff.

If sponsors have enough endurance, they can sometimes pass a bill by having so many drafting sessions and so many rewrites that opponents lose interest, wear out, or decide their opposition has reached a point of diminishing returns. Opponents must win concessions so they have a basis to rationalize giving up the fight, of course. Otherwise they get as stubborn as the sponsors. The name of this game is "Wear the bastards down."

§ 20–2. Limit scope. If a bill is drafted to be passed, it must be drafted to ruffle as few feathers as possible. If from the beginning, coverage is limited to the prime targets, sponsors will face a smaller corps of opponents. A later tactical amendment to narrow the coverage of a bill will not help the bill's passage as much as conservative drafting in the first place. What the sponsors seek is peace on one flank. If an opponent sees that other interests can win exemption from the bill while the full impact still falls on his group, he will fight more vigorously and can make the effective point that his client is being discriminated against. To let some groups off the hook is no compromise to those left on the hook. Furthermore, lobbyists threatened by a bill may agree at an early date to stick together even if some of their clients are amended out of the bill's coverage. Those groups which will be left out in the end ought to be omitted in the first place so they do not join a pact to unite in opposition.

The best compromise is one which leaves those who are subject to the bill semi-mollified and convinced that the bill sponsors acted as fairly as possible in pursuing their objective. Occasionally a bill is intentionally drawn so there is room for compromise; that is, it is made unnecessarily strong to establish a tougher starting point for bargaining. But there is no reason to make its coverage unnecessarily broad, for effective compromise must be with those who in the end are subject to the bill's provisions.

§ 20–3. Intentional vagueness. Some provisions of a bill can be drawn (1) so the bill sponsors lose something they would like to achieve, (2) so the sponsors achieve their whole objective, even though to do so will spark vigorous opposition, or (3) so a critical issue is left up in the air. Which choice should a sponsor select? The first gives him an easier job. Opponents are less aroused. He leaves part of his battle for a later day. The second choice gives him some trading stock for compromise. If he can pass the bill with the provision in, he wins a more significant victory. But the bill may not pass. The third choice makes his bill incomplete. It may bother those who want certainty in the law. He may lose when the issue is later decided in court. On the other hand, vagueness may cause those affected to overlook the additional hazard in the bill or to decide they are willing to gamble on winning the later decision. The sponsor then faces milder opposition and a simpler legislative battle.

There is no one correct choice, but the third option, intentional vagueness, serves legislatures well and often. It may be adopted consciously by a draftsman, occur by oversight, or turn up as a compromise during negotiation on the bill. A legislature eagerly ducks a tough question if answering that question threatens the passage of a bill for which a consensus has developed.

§ 20–4. Half bills. On many problems, political timeliness and legislative desire to act outrun
the intellectual raw material available. This may
arise when a rule of law becomes discredited, but
no substitute is supported broadly enough to win
legislative approval. To respond, the legislature
may pass a bill which cancels the old rule, leaving
it to the judiciary to fill the newly created blank
in the law. For example, judicial precedents and
statutes establish the rule that in the sale of real
property the only implied warranty is good title.
The legislature may want to open the way to
warranties on fitness of the property for the use
intended. But the legislature may be unready to
spell out the types of properties and sales to be
included, the remedies, the circumstances in whch
there is a right to contract out of implied warranties, and the obligation of a buyer to inspect
the property for himself. So the bill may provide
only: "In the sale of real property, warranties in
addition to a warranty of good title may be implied to the extent appropriate." This bill re-
moves the barrier of the old law and allows the
courts to develop the specifics of a new and better law.

A more common legislative response to a major
problem for which no legislative solution is
known is this simplistic approach: the legislature
describes the problem, it declares the problem
will be met, and it establishes an agency for envi-

ronmental protection, energy management, or mass transit to do the job. Constitutents cannot say the legislature ignored the problem, although that is about what it did. Sometimes this frightening abdication of responsibility may even work.

§ 20–5. Packaging bills. In most jurisdictions bills must relate to a single subject. But a broad title can gather under one subject a multitude of provisions. Tactical packaging of legislative work in general appropriation bills, omnibus bills, housekeeping bills, law revisions, form revisions or recodifications is an art of high value. So is shrewd use of packets of related bills or one-line bills or repealers. The housekeeping bill is an especially interesting device. It is pages long. Section after section improve grammar and style, correct obvious errors, adjust agency fees to match inflation, and so on. But deep in the bill some section may insert a few words with implications worth careful thought. These hidden substantive provisions are called woodchucks by their victims.

Over the long haul, legislative tacticians do best by packaging legislation in honest bills without woodchucks. Earned trust passes bills. When sponsors have both substantive and technical objectives, separating the provisions into two bills is often helpful. The technical provisions are offered and accepted on a faith basis; the

sponsor can concentrate his educational and persuasive work on the substantive bill. A single
bill forces readers to search for substance in sections where none exists. The whole package,
when divided into two bills, seems less weighty
than one all-purpose bill.

Putting each substantive change into a separate bill also may be a good tactic, even if they
could be combined in one bill. The sponsor must
evaluate the support and opposition to each separate objective. He must determine whether combining the changes builds a consensus of support
or accumulates opposition. He must decide
whether lukewarm legislators will take the bad
with the good or reject the good because of the
bad. He must also look ahead to judge the likeli-
hood that he can pass the toughest pieces of his
program at some future time without the attrac-
tions of its other parts. The efficient use of the
sponsor's time is also a consideration. Handling
a number of small bills is usually more work than
handling a single large bill.

Sometimes using the extra long bill pays divi-
dends. When a bill reaches a certain length, it
intimidates the legislature. Legislators look for a
consensus among the interest groups affected instead of giving the bill independent review. The
Uniform Commercial Code passed most legislatures with the support of a united commercial
community. With no one raising serious objec-

tion, most legislators happily skipped any meaningful study of the bill for it contained almost 100,000 words. They took it on faith.

Measured by the effort expended against the results achieved, long bills are highly efficient. Measured by the amount of thought and knowledge brought to bear on each legal change, long bills are less likely to produce sound legislative judgments, however. Sponsors do well to use long bills when they can, but legislators and others sitting in review must allocate time according to the substance of the bill. This will lead to more study of multi-page bills. The one-paragraph bill gets many times the attention per word given to longer bills. Logically a bill with twenty-five substantive sections should get as much attention as twenty-five single-section bills, but legislatures do not work that way.

When a long bill is being reviewed, attention lags before review is complete. Since almost everyone reads bills starting at section one, closing sections rarely receive the attention of an alert mind. The sponsor may take advantage of this fact by hiding a sensitive or unpopular section near the end of a bill, rather than putting it where logical organization might dictate.

PART III

PERSPECTIVES ON LEGISLATIVE POWER

CHAPTER 6

LEGISLATIVE POLICY MAKING

A. SOURCES OF LEGISLATIVE POWER

§ 21–1. **States—residual power.** The republican system of government means legislative power resides in an elected representative body. Legislative power is the authority to make public policy through the enactment of statutes. The legislative body derives its power from the constitution of the jurisdiction it serves. All state constitutions contain a provision creating a legislative branch. Having established a legislature, a state constitution need go no further. There naturally falls to that institution all the legislative power of the state. Any additional words regarding legislative power are superfluous or limit the legislature in some way. A state constitution is consulted only to find limitations on legislative power; an affirmative grant of power as authority for any specific piece of legislation is unnecessary.

This republican form of government (representative democracy) is not only the form of the federal government, but also is imposed by the United States constitution upon states as a condition of membership in the union.

§ 21–2. Congress—delegated powers. Congressional power differs fundamentally from state legislative power. The federal Congress possesses only those powers which have been delegated to it by the states. Each act of Congress must be founded on some power granted in the United States constitution. In preparing legislation for the United States Congress, the underlying constitutional grant of authority is often explicitly identified. The tenth amendment to the federal constitution reads: "The powers not delegated to the United States by the Constitution nor prohibited by it to the states, are reserved to the states, respectively, or to the people." This amendment makes it clear that Congress possesses only delegated powers.

Another clause dramatically expands the granted powers of Congress. Article I, Sec. 8, clause 18, says Congress has power "To make all laws which shall be necessary and proper for carrying into execution the foregoing powers, and all other powers vested by this Constitution in the government of the United States, or in any department or officer thereof." With this as its bootstrap,

Congress has found legal justification for nearly anything it wanted to enact. Courts have grown accustomed to finding that acts of Congress are necessary and proper to implement some granted power.

§ 21–3. Local units—delegated powers. Legislative power also resides in municipal councils, school boards, county commissioner boards, and boards for other units of local government. Local governments derive their power from specific state constitutional provisions or from legislation delegating responsibility for policy making on certain issues. Local ordinances or resolutions must be based on specific grants of power in the state constitution or in state legislation; local units, like Congress, possess only those powers delegated to them.

B.   CHARACTER OF LEGISLATIVE LAW

§ 22–1. Statutory law. Rules of law, whether made by court or legislature, represent public policy. Legislatures continually make and remake legal rules as they work to shape public policy to reflect current knowledge and values. The dynamic character of legislative lawmaking challenges lawyers to aid clients and the public by participating in the legislative process, rather than accepting legislative law as is.

Still, as a lawyer advises clients on what the law is, he must turn to the statute books, not to a bill drafter. No matter what field a lawyer works in, legislative law is dominant. In commercial law the Uniform Commercial Code is the primary source of legal rules. Consumer protection acts are significant in affecting the operation of the market place. The law of marriage and divorce comes from the legislature. Legislation provides the basic rules for criminal law, probate administration, securities and corporate law, debtor's and creditor's rights. Benefits under welfare programs, medicare, and vocational rehabilitation are set and administered pursuant to legislative action. The more specialized fields of law—labor law, local government law, patent law, bankruptcy law, anti-trust law—are built primarily on legislation. Compensation under workmen's compensation is based on statute. Federal and state administrative procedure acts provide the foundation for the processes of administrative law. Even in the ancient field of property law, acts providing for recording systems and acts modifying old common law principles in landlord-tenant relationships significantly affect the law.

This list of legal fields dominated by legislation establishes that legislatures are the pre-eminent lawmaking institutions of our society. The proposition can stand, even omitting the pervasive impact of tax legislation on the conduct of personal and business activities.

§ 22–2. Statutory rule equals case rule.

Many lawyers carry a distorted impression of legislative law, despite its omnipresence in daily life. Practitioner and scholar view rules made by legislative bodies as different from rules derived from appellate court precedents—as more authoritative, more rigid, more meddlesome, less lawyerly. A sounder understanding is Judge Vinson's ". . . the law is all the law there is, the law is more for the parties than for the courts, the people will rely upon and adjust their behavior in accordance with all the law *be it legislative or judicial or both.*" (Warring v. Colpoys, 122 F.2d 642 (1941)).

Judicial and legislative law speak to society with equal authority; both are backed by sanctions, both are subject to change to account for new conditions and new wisdom. The law from each institution is often modified by the other. Both are forward looking in their impact. Lawmaking is a partnership of court and legislature.

Legislatures make broad general rules carrying the law in new directions. Legislatures, through the process of codification, also organize and streamline and thus simplify the law. In these tasks, legislative bodies possess significant advantages. They have available resources for research which may produce several volumes of background on a single legislative proposal. To the judicial system falls the task of lawmaking in the context of actual fact situations. A court makes law with hindsight. Lawmaking by judicial precedent, our system of common law, has demonstrated the great capacity of courts to recognize what is just in the context of a particular controversy. Making a fair rule for the case at hand produces a just precedent for the future. In the partnership of court and legislature, the judicial branch refines the generalizations of the legislature, fills the blanks in legislative enactments, and incorporates into the lawmaking mechanism the basic values embodied in constitutions, which on occasion are overlooked in the pressures of legislative conflict.

Historically, greater resources of intellect have been devoted to the judicial lawmaking function. Society has not allocated adequate intellectual resources to the legislative branch. The partnership could work better if more attention were paid to legislative lawmaking.

§ 22–3. **Statute as precedent.** A slow evolution is occurring in the common law partnership of court and legislature, an evolution prompted by a growing appreciation of the civil law system of continental Europe. Under civil law, legislation provides principles from which courts generalize to decide cases. Common law courts can, in the same way, use legislative enactments as precedents justifying change from prior common law decisions. This use of statutes was vigorously advocated by Dean Roscoe Pound as early as 1908 (Pound, *Common Law and Legislation* 21 Harv.L.Rev. 383). What Dean Pound urged in 1908 received Supreme Court recognition in Justice Harlan's concurring opinion in the 1970 conscientious objector case of Welch v. United States (90 S.Ct. 1792). In his opinion, Justice Harlan found defendant Welch to be outside the coverage of the conscientious objector statute, but he found in the logic of the statute justification for granting Welch a draft exemption under the court's lawmaking authority. Justice Harlan used the legislative enactment as the wellspring for a common law ruling. Whether Harlan's opinion will accelerate the evolution toward a broader civil law approach in the United States remains to be seen.

The usual approach of common law lawyers and courts to a statute is to examine the description of the persons and circumstances to which the rule is to be applied. If the parties are not included within the statutory clauses or if the circumstances are outside the statute, the court assumes an intent to exclude the case from the reach of the statute. This negative inference, which may have no logical basis, blocks the court from developing a common law rule consistent with the act. This habit of statutory interpretation means the legislative act can make no contribution to the evolution of the law. In fact it is counterproductive.

§ 22–4. Rigidity of statute law. In the partnership of court and legislature, the legislature contributes the most dramatic changes in the law; but it also has a serious stultifying effect on specific rules. The rigidity of statute law arises first from the tendency of the legislature to ignore a field of law once it has enacted a basic code in the area. It is difficult for those who seek to reform old legislative enactments in the private law area to get the attention of the legislature. That attention is more likely to go to the issues of appropriation, taxation, and government operation. The work of past legislatures in the fields of property law, probate law, commercial law, patent law, bankruptcy law, securities law, and other unpolitical or private law fields are not reexamined with appropriate regularity.

The second factor contributing to rigidity in statutory law results from the lawmaking prerogatives of court and legislature. The legislature holds basic policy-making authority. When a statute is enacted, courts are restricted in their authority to impose a conflicting policy viewpoint. A court may find itself forced to adhere to the clear policy of the statute even though this produces an unjust result. In other words, when the legislature has acted in a field of law, the judicial system may be foreclosed from law reform which would otherwise come through judicial decisions. The converse is not the case. If a judicial decision has left a defect in the law, that defect is subject to legislative or judicial correction. Legislative action in a field theoretically reduces by half the opportunity to reform the law and forces on courts the obsolete policy judgments of a legislative body. Courts quite effectively escape this theoretical trap, however. Using constitutional principles, courts set aside a share of legislative errors. In other cases, courts read statutes both to produce justice in the case before them and to modify statute law so that it accords with current knowledge and necessity. If judges fully appreciated the obstacles to legislative reform of private law, they would provide more imaginative statutory interpretation to strengthen the lawmaking partnership of court and legislature. Lawyers, as advocates in court, ought to encourage this progressive treatment of legislative acts.

C. FORM OF LEGISLATIVE LAW

§ 23–1. Acts and session laws. A bill which makes its way completely through the legislative process is filed by the chief executive with the secretary of state. The filed copy, called the enrolled bill, is the most authoritative source of the statutory law in a jurisdiction. After the annual or biennial legislative session, each jurisdiction publishes books of session laws in which acts appear as chapters numbered in the order they were filed with the secretary of state. These volumes are entitled "Laws of (*State*) 19___." The session laws of the United States Congress are entitled "United States Statutes at Large, ___ Congress, First (or Second) Session." At the municipal level, ordinances are generally filed with a city or village clerk and published in a legal newspaper. Copies of single acts or ordinances are available from various offices.

§ 23–2. Compilations. A shelf of books containing the laws enacted by each legislative session since the founding of a state includes all the statutory law of that jurisdiction. But to make legislative law usable it must be published in a form that groups together all currently effective provisions on each topic. For example, provisions relating to traffic laws, no matter when passed, must be included in one chapter and placed in logical order. This publication is called a statutory compilation. Although extremely helpful, only a handful of states publish an official compilation. In these states, it is done every few years by an officer of the state with the title

Revisor of Statutes or Code Revisor. These compilations contain the general and permanent statutory law of the jurisdiction and reflect all legislative changes up to the date of publication.

A significant benefit of official compilation is that the legislature may amend the law by reference to the compilation. The procedure followed in states without up-to-date official compilation is to refer in amending legislation to the original enactment and to all subsequent amendments. When the amendment is to a provision of the law which has been frequently amended, the result is a bill nearly impossible to understand. Despite obvious advantages, universal acceptance of regular official compilation has been blocked by two obstacles. First, a large investment is required to produce the initial compilation; and second, the annual cost is high to maintain an office of the professional quality needed to keep the compilation current session after session.

§ 23–3. **Annotated statutes.** Private law book publishers produce compilations to make the statutory law readily available in states with and without official compilations. Lawyers, courts, and legislatures treat these unofficial compilations as the source books for the statutory law of the state. The unofficial compilations take on the character of official compilations in everyday life.

To make their compilations more useful, private publishers add annotations referring to relevant judicial precedents, law review articles, attorney general opinions, and legislative histories. Annotated statutes are a primary tool for legal research in states both with and without official compilations. Sets of annotated statutes are published for all fifty states, the District of Columbia, Puerto Rico and the Virgin Islands. The United States Code Annotated is a comparable publication covering the acts of the United States Congress.

§ 23–4. **Law revisions.** From time to time legislatures undertake law improvement efforts called law revisions. A law revision is a single act repealing and reenacting the entire statutory law on a particular topic or on all topics. If all the legislative law of the state is involved, it is called a bulk revision; if one subject is involved, it is called a topical revision. Revision starts with a compilation. The compilation, rather than merely being published, is brought to the legislature as a bill which the legislature affirmatively enacts. The pre-existing acts from which the compilation is constructed are repealed. The adoption of revised laws is the essential first step in instituting a system of official continuous compilation. But even if a jurisdiction misses the opportunity to begin continual official compilation, the housecleaning involved in the adoption of revised laws is probably essential at least twice each century.

Law revision can be substantive or can be limited to organization and style. In the first, the rules of the statutory law are updated. In the second, the effort is limited to improving the form of the law by eliminating duplicate and obsolete provisions and by organizing the acts adopted by the legislature over the years in orderly chapters, sections, and sub-sections, without changing their substantive effect.

§ 23–5. Codification. Complicating the vocabulary of legislation is the activity of codification. Codification is distinguished from law revision because it always involves substantive change in the law and because it not only reworks the jurisdiction's statutory law but also puts into the statutes relevant rules of law derived from judicial precedent. A code is a systematic and comprehensive statement of all the principal rules of law in a particular field adopted as an act of the legislature. Great achievements in law improvement have been accomplished by codification because the process blends the output of both lawmaking institutions in our society—the judiciary and the legislature. Examples of significant codifications are the Uniform Commercial Code, corporate codes, probate codes, criminal codes, motor vehicle codes, and administrative procedure acts.

CHAPTER 7

GOVERNING BY LEGISLATURES

A. LEGISLATURE AS OPERATOR OF GOVERNMENT

§ 24–1. Creating and financing government agencies. A constitution provides the broad charter for the organization of government. The task of completing the organization falls to the legislative branch. The executive branch agencies are created by legislative act; reorganizing and updating these agencies is a constant legislative activity. In addition, the legislature usually has responsibility for the judicial tribunals, including municipal, probate, juvenile, county, family, general trial, and appellate courts.

After it establishes the structure of government, the legislature must appropriate funds to keep the machinery operating. Budgets of executive-administrative agencies depend upon legislative appropriations or upon fees authorized by legislative act. Within the legislative institution, the appropriation task consumes more energy than any other. The power of the purse insures that bureaucrats of the executive branch, over time, are extremely sensitive to the opinions of the legislative branch. In a power struggle between the elected executive and the legislative branch, the government bureaucracy is as much an ally of the legislature as of the executive. The executive may claim loyalty from his appointees and those who hope for future appointments, but the legislature has as allies the career employees who are permanently dependent on appropriations.

§ 24–2. Legislative oversight. The legislature carries an obligation to oversee the work of government agencies. The basic oversight function is carried out in the appropriating process, where the performances of agencies are examined and evaluated against their requests for financial support. Oversight is not all concerned with money, however. Legislative hearings on proposals to change missions, to reorganize, and to alter procedures enable legislatures to examine the performance of agencies. Senate confirmation of an executive appointee also provides an occasion for legislative oversight; the appointee may be examined about his attitudes on the agency's mission and his plans to accomplish the objectives of the agency.

Legislative oversight may occur when a legislator provides service to constituents. After receiving a complaint, a legislator contacts the agency for an accounting of its actions. Agency performance may improve as a result. The agen-

cy is more likely to respond simply by accommo-
dating the interests of the person who contacted
the legislator. The underlying practices which
led to the dissatisfaction may not be corrected.
Though the legislator's immediate problem of an
unhappy constituent is met, the legislator usually
lacks the sophistication, the energy, or the moti-
vation to remedy the underlying deficiencies. In
fact, when a legislator's contact with the agency
leads to favored treatment for his constituent, his
intervention may weaken total agency performance, rather than improve it.

§ 24–3. **Local government supervision.** State
legislatures establish the pattern of local government organization and finance. The forms and
powers of municipalities, the role of counties, the
method of school district organization all depend
upon legislation. Special service districts and re-
gional government agencies represent legislative
decisions. Programs of state aids (state taxes re-
distributed to local governments) provide significant municipal and school money. In addition,
local taxing power comes from legislative authorization and is subject to whatever restrictions
the legislature imposes.

B. LEGISLATURE AS ALLOCATOR OF RESOURCES

§ 25–1. Money and public policy. A valid criticism of legislative performance is that legislatures fail to control the use of society's resources with appropriate energy, courage and long-range perspective. Money issues—levying taxes and making appropriations—come close to dominating legislative work, but little external help is offered except that motivated by direct selfish interest.

Whether decisions on spending are expressed as reordering of priorities, meeting public needs, saving the taxpayers' dollars or any of the other taxing-spending phrases of politics, these decisions are a significant legislative function. In 1973 an estimated twenty-two percent of the gross national product was expended at the direction of national, state, and local legislative bodies. The public policy ramifications of the decisions behind these expenditures are profound. Major social impacts arise from both spending and taxing.

§ 25–2. Appropriations. There are a myriad of policy judgments involved in decisions which allocate resources. Are schools to be financed locally, or through state aids? Will rich districts offer better programs or will all districts offer equal opportunities? Are public colleges to be fi-

[*164*]

nanced at a level which allows modest tuition and quality education, thus squeezing private colleges to a smaller and smaller share of the educational market place? Are student aids to be provided to subsidize private colleges indirectly? Are public institutions for the retarded and the mentally ill to be financed at custodial levels? Or will appropriations include funds for treatment and for training? Are appropriations going to be made to preserve nature areas? Will public resources be made available for playgrounds, parks, zoos? Will the quality of these facilities be good or bad? Are public resources to be directed at speeding the automobile from home to job, or for mass transit? Will public funds go to train police, or to produce a corrections system designed to pull the apprehended criminal from his criminal life style? Will health money be spent on treatment, or on preventive medicine, public health, and medical research?

§ 25–3. **Taxation.** Every dollar appropriated by legislative bodies is extracted from the public through tax legislation. Tax policies have significant potential for social engineering. For example, the level of death taxes affects the degree of concentration of wealth. Selective excise taxes penalize the product taxed. Taxes on business, passed on as part of the price, produce a regressive tax structure. Reliance on income taxes creates a tax structure less attractive to the wealthy. Policy choices in income tax provisions also involve social engineering. Examples are special treatment for capital gains, deductions for charitable contributions, exemptions for senior citizens, credits for dependent children, investment credits and depletion allowances.

The hardest fought battle in the average legislative session occurs on the omnibus revenue-raising bill. The public policy made in that bill may be short term, or it may set a pattern of taxation that will continue for decades. Either way, the decisions involve millions of dollars. While the bill is written and re-written, those who will have to pay can and do calculate the cost. As tax legislation is negotiated, lobbyists for tobacco, liquor, mining, retail, wholesale, utility and manufacturing industries lose a great deal of sleep as they play their separate or cooperative roles in influencing the final bill.

C. LEGISLATURE AS INVESTIGATOR

§ 26–1. The tool of investigation. The legislative investigation is a basic means for carrying forward legislative work. The investigation may be a straight-forward hearing (an ordinary step in the legislative process) or it may be a strong pursuit of new information relevant to policy making.

In addition to its use in lawmaking, resource allocation, and government operation, legislative investigation has a function of its own—public education. The massive records developed by congressional committees often lead to decisive turns in public policy. They provide the raw material for reporters, editorial writers, muckrakers, scholars, and the policy formulators from business, labor, and agriculture organizations. Legislative investigations have revealed abuses not being exposed in any other arena. Hearings on war profiteering by the Truman committee and those on the Wall Street abuses which contributed to the Great Depression are examples of investigations that clearly had affirmative benefits.

§ 26–2. Investigative abuses; safeguards. Like any other power, the legislative power to investigate can be abused. To many people, these investigations are synonymous with witch-hunts. Finding scapegoats is a classic political technique in both totalitarian and democratic societies. Legislators are politicians and an investigation is a way to use the scapegoat device, if a legislator is so inclined. The best safeguard against abuse of the power to investigate is good sense and responsible attitudes in the legislature. There also are constitutional due process restraints. The leading case is Watkins v. United States (77 S.Ct. 1173 (1957)) which laid down the following rules for the protection of any person caught up in a legislative investigation.

 *The investigation must relate to a subject upon which the legislature can act.

 *The resolution authorizing the investigation must define with specificity the scope of the investigation.

 *The proceedings must accord with defined standards of due process.

 *The legislative right to be informed must outweigh a witness's right of privacy.

 *The privilege against self-incrimination must be respected.

 *Unreasonable search and seizure is prohibited.

 *The freedoms of speech, press, religion, or political belief and association cannot be abridged.

In evaluating legislative investigations, it helps to recall that witch-hunting Senator Joseph McCarthy, after his abuse of the investigative power, was brought down by that same power in the Army-McCarthy hearings of 1953.

§ 26–3. Legislature versus executive. A legislative investigation may conflict with a claim of executive privilege based on the need for confidentiality necessary for the executive branch to effectively and efficiently perform its functions. Operation of the executive requires some confidentiality of internal advice and discussion (work product) and protection of sources of information. Courts are reluctant to enter into disputes between executive and legislative branches over the issue of executive privilege. Such disputes are usually left to the political process for resolution.

In United States v. Nixon, (94 S.Ct. 3090 (1974)) the court ruled judicial intervention is appropriate and claims of executive privilege must give way to the need for evidence when what is involved is "due process of law in the fair administration of criminal justice." But dicta in the opinion supported significant executive privilege, and as a precedent the case may weaken the legislative branch in its capacity to investigate the executive. However, political reality deters executives from non-cooperation and may prove to be more compelling than any legal refuge gained from U. S. v. Nixon. That case is not likely to be a popular citation for public relations aides with the responsibility to protect the reputation of any chief executive—president, governor or mayor.

CHAPTER 8

LIMITATIONS ON LEGISLATIVE POWER

A. PRACTICAL LIMITATIONS ON LEGISLATIVE POWER

§ 27-1. **Legislative frustration.** A legislature at work is conscious of legal limitations on legislative power, but is more conscious of real-life restraints on what it can do about the problems of society. External disillusionment with the institution is often based on a misunderstanding of what the legislature can accomplish. Failures are blamed on an absence of good intentions, rather than on an absence of practical ideas. While critics condemn the lack of response to particular problems, those same critics fail to help the legislature overcome barriers to effective action. The legislator is frustrated by his inability to meet society's aspirations and also by the public cynicism which greets this inability.

§ 27-2. **Political reality as a limitation.** Most voters suffer ambivalent feelings as to whether they want their elected representative to be responsive to the demands of constituents or whether they want him to be courageous and independent, deciding each issue on the merits without worrying about reelection. Often a voter avoids this question by thinking his legislator can do both these things if he just votes the way the voter tells him to. People associate and talk politics most often with others who have the same background and are therefore likely to hold similar political views. This leads people to believe that their opinions are majority positions and that a legislator who disagrees is both wrong and unresponsive.

A legislative candidate who wants to be elected usually does not declare his intention to vote his convictions regardless of popular opinion. Nonetheless, the legislator who votes on most issues in accord with his own judgment is common. There are several reasons legislators do not simply follow public opinion. First, a mistrust of opinion polls and the accuracy of letter-writing campaigns as gauges of public opinion is endemic among legislators. Second, the legislator learns quickly that he can defend an honestly cast vote even to a constituent who disagrees with it. Most voters tolerate a thoughtfully defended position even if it is contrary to their own. Third, a legislative vote is seldom a political issue in a later campaign. The electorate looks ahead to future issues. Fourth, voters pass judgment more on the candidate than on the issues. Voting for the best man and for a party candidate are the most common—and the most intelligent—election-day practices. Issues come and go, but the winning candidate stays to vote on many other questions. Opportunists are more often elected to public office in issue-oriented campaigns than in campaigns where the candidates square off on the question of who is the better person.

Most legislators do not walk the corridors of capitols trembling with concern over their next campaign. But they worry. Most legislators trim their sails on some issues. The sail trimming, coupled with the fact that members usually hold the same biases as their constituents, mean the institution seldom acts on a controversial issue until a solid consensus develops in the general public. The conservatism of public opinion acts as a significant limitation on the actions and power of legislatures. This political reality hobbles the institution in its support for those who would strike boldly in new directions. Groups frustrated by this characteristic do not admit that it is actually political responsiveness which defeats their objectives. They blame instead legislative senility, stupidity, unresponsiveness, or, even worse, legislative venality.

This section addresses a fundamental issue of political theory: the validity of Edmund Burke's view of the legislator as a representative using "his unbiased opinion, his mature judgment, his enlightened conscience" free of dictation from his constituents. Burke provides the material for

rich theoretical discussion. The practical conclu-
sion, however, is that legislators (and a legislature as a whole) follow Burke—when they dare.

§ 27–3. Inadequate sanctions. Even if the
legislature wants to act and has a favorable political climate in which to act, it may not be able to
solve a problem. The failure of prohibition between 1919 and 1933 is a reminder that a legislature cannot force people out of their usual pattern of behavior. Citizens cannot be coerced to
virtue. Legislating morals may serve as an expression of community consensus, but legislators
and legal scholars have not discovered sanctions
to push people into conduct they are not ready to
follow. When legislatures attempt to dictate
morals, the law is embarrassed if there is non-
compliance. It is also weakened, because the dignity and legitimacy of compliance are vital to its
strength.

The American Bar Association has recommended repeal of statutes against victimless
crimes. Whether there are victims or not may
be the practical key to whether state intervention
on moral issues is wise. Prohibiting an activity
when no one else is affected has little consequence except to reduce respect for the law. On
the other hand, the law can tackle conduct based
on the deepest prejudices and most established
conventions when that conduct hurts other citi-

zens. Dignity and legitimacy are present when
the law seeks to protect those who need protection, and no amount of evasion of the law can
take that dignity away. Many of those who urge
repeal of victimless crime laws support anti-dis-
crimination legislation. In the first case, violation of the law makes repeal sensible; in the second case, violation makes enforcement necessary.

§ 27–4. **Inadequate legal mechanisms.** Legislative policy must be implemented through the
executive and judicial branches of government.
Closely coupled with the inadequacy of sanctions
is the absence of legal mechanisms in the other
branches to enforce sanctions or to otherwise accomplish the objectives of legislative policy.
Prosecutors often are unwilling to charge and
juries are unwilling to convict. Administrative
agencies are reluctant to act when there is significant resistance. Agencies and courts cannot discover facts necessary to support enforcement action. The deficiencies and handicaps of those
who must enforce the law—inherent or arising
from inadequacies of talent or will—undercut legislative policy objectives. Bureaucratic red tape
and arbitrariness, weak executives and prosecutors, court delay, and the co-opted regulatory
agency explain why legislatures cannot effectively harness the power of society to produce the results sought through legislative enactments.

§ 27–5. Inadequate financial resources. Money is required to achieve many legislative objectives. Providing health care, education, highways, welfare, consumer protection, scientific research, historic preservation, environmental protection and other programs add up to a financial burden of great magnitude. Added to these are the tax burdens of national defense and such local government programs as police and fire protection, water and sewer service, and traffic regulation.

While the public supports these objectives and supports legislators who pass programs to achieve them, they also resist increased taxes to pay for them; there is constant pressure to hold down taxes. Legislators convert that voter pressure into legislative resistance to expenditure; for political survival they must say no to some expenditures. Limited financial resources stop a legislature from doing many things it would like to do. A legislature can do no more than use society's resources wisely, while at the same time responding pragmatically to political pressures.

§ 27–6. Inadequate knowledge, imagination, wisdom. "Knowledge is power," according to Francis Bacon. The legislature, together with other human institutions, struggles along with imperfect knowledge. Because of this limitation, it can never exercise its full theoretical potential.

The legislature does not receive information which exists elsewhere in the community. Facts may not reach the legislative body because they are purposefully held back, because no interest group communicates them, because there is no appreciation of their potential value to the legislature, or because citizens lack knowledge about how to provide the information in usable form. The legislature also shares the ignorance of the rest of society. What doctors do not know about health hazards, what environmentalists do not know about environmental impacts, what economists do not know about economic interrelationships is not known by the legislature either.

Another intellectual deficiency of legislatures is lack of imagination. Americans have a history of mechanical ingenuity; their inventions have changed the economic life of the world. Invention has a role in the legislative process. Somebody has to work out legislative solutions to recognized problems. Until the ingenious idea comes, the legislative institution cannot act, no matter how clear the necessity for action may be. Our legal inventions have never matched our scientific and mechanical developments.

Finally, there is the element of wisdom. The job of the legislature—passing judgment on proposals for legislation—requires common sense and a long perspective. This quality of wisdom is

not universal in or out of legislative bodies; legislatures are human institutions with human failings.

§ 27–7. **Time and pay.** Limitations arising
from intellectual failings are compounded because
of time pressures. Legislators are universally
over-burdened with legislative and political responsibilities. When a session adjourns, a legislator looks back on dozens of decisions which required more study and thought than he was able
to give to them. Every legislator at every level
is reminded of this time pressure by the stack of
reports he has not read, laws he voted on without
adequate study, by the number of agencies and
public institutions he has not visited and whose
functions he does not fully understand.

Most state constitutions limit the length of legislative sessions, although through amendment
and changing customs, periods of meeting are
being extended dramatically. Between 1960 and
1974, states with annual sessions increased from
twenty to forty-two. Official times for meeting
tell only part of the story because interim work
through special commissions or standing committees can produce year-round legislative activity.
The real limit on time is the salary level. Legislative work must compete for time with career
and family obligations. When legislators are
paid part-time salaries, they give part-time serv-

ice. States do not pay legislative salaries that justify full-time vocational commitments from individuals with the level of ability required to be excellent legislators.

B. LEGAL LIMITATIONS ON LEGISLATIVE POWER

§ 28–1. Bill of rights limitations. Constitutions, especially bill of rights sections, limit legislative power. Bills of rights, state and federal, have a significant impact on legislative life. They are an invaluable bulwark against the more irrational proposals made to legislative institutions. For example, they protect private property rights. The provision that private property cannot be taken without just compensation appropriately and directly frustrates many legislative aspirations; that provision protects individual owners by making it necessary for legislatures to appropriate funds to acquire park land, confiscate billboards, save redwoods, obtain highway rights-of-way, clear slum property and achieve many other valuable goals. The requirements of due process of law and equal protection are also pervasive obstacles to inappropriate legislative action.

Prohibitions on *ex post facto* laws and bills of attainder are bill of rights provisions aimed directly at legislative action. An *ex post facto* law makes conduct criminal or increases the applicable penalty after the conduct has occurred. Bills of attainder are legislative pronouncements of guilt, imposing a sanction on identified individuals without judicial process.

§ 28–2. General constitutional limitations. The following are examples of common constitutional restraints on legislative power beyond bill of rights limitations. Each may or may not exist in a state.

(a) *Special legislation:* Special legislation is often barred by a generality like: "No special legislation shall be passed where a general law may be made applicable." In other states the limitation prohibits particular types of special legislation or combines a general limitation and more precise proscriptions. These limitations respond to a timeless problem in all state legislatures—the practice of passing acts applicable to specific localities or to limited circumstances. This practice leads to ill-considered policies, favoritism, legislator domination of local government, and waste of legislative energies.

(b) *Taxing power:* The authority to impose taxes is prescribed in state constitutions in a variety of ways. These may be sound, simple requirements that taxes be uniform on the same class of taxpayers. Or they may be complex, detailed provisions establishing special taxation for railroads, extractive industries, motor vehicles, forest products, newly-established business, homesteads, or eleemosynary institutions. Any tax bill passed by a legislature must be written with these limitations in mind.

(c) *Dedicated funds:* Proceeds from particular taxes may be dedicated by a constitution to specific uses. Sometimes the rationale is that the tax is primarily a user fee, as is the case with the dedication of motor vehicle and gasoline taxes to road building. Other times the repercussion from a new tax is cushioned by dedicating the proceeds to a politically attractive use like reforestation. A legislature at a later date may want to use the funds for a more timely and appropriate purpose. The legislative craftsman may be able to label as reforestation, activities which are only marginally related, if there is a legislative consensus to bypass the constitutional limitation. Technical ingenuity and judicial reluctance to set aside actions of the popularly-elected legislative branch usually permit the legislature to have its way. But it is difficult to build a legislative consensus in the face of restrictive constitutional provisions.

(d) *Debt limits:* Legislative profligacy has led to constitutional restrictions on the legislative power to incur debt. These limitations may be expressed in dollar figures. Where this is the case, the provisions are repealed or evaded as inflation makes them absurd. In other jurisdictions the use of borrowed funds is restricted to capital expenditures, or an extraordinary vote within the legislative body is required to incur debt.

(e) *Grandfather provisions:* When the state constitutions were written, particular aspects of the *status quo* occasionally were protected. University or college charters, state capital locations, or county lines may have constitutional status. These touch-me-not provisions may conflict with desired legislative policy decades after their adoption. Again, drafting ingenuity can achieve legislative objectives while avoiding direct conflict with the literal words of these provisions.

(f) *Mandated programs:* State constitutions may require the legislature to maintain a militia, to establish public schools, and to carry out a variety of other programs. If a recalcitrant legislature ignores a constitutionally imposed obligation, the legal system provides no sanction to force its implementation. The constitutional provision does give legislative strength to those who support the mandated program, however. When the constitution imposes the obligation to implement a program on an executive branch official, a mandamus action may be brought to require that the program be carried on. But the official and the court will be stymied if the legislature fails to appropriate money to meet the obligation.

[*181*]

Whether a program is constitutionally mandated or not, the appropriation power gives the legislature a means to cut it off if it chooses. Even if the provision of the constitution includes dedicated appropriations from state revenues, the level of expenditure must be left to legislative discretion. The legislature can respond with a dollar-a-year program.

§ 28–3. **State boundary.** A multitude of activities that a legislature would like to regulate occur beyond its territorial jurisdiction. These events may involve drinking or marrying or contracting at an age lower than is permitted in the home state. They may involve statutory authority for the organization of corporations under a set of rules contrary to the policy of the home state. Conflict with the policies of other states is an everyday limitation on many business-climate issues. Not being able to control public policy in other jurisdictions, a state must continually act with one eye on the realities of interstate competition faced by its domestic businesses, including the costs of unemployment and workman's compensation, pollution control, minimum wages, taxes, and neglected public services.

§ 28–4. **Past and future as limitations.** Law contemplates a citizenry aware of what legal rules are day by day. This means that once a day has passed into history, the lawmakers—

courts or legislature—are restricted in their freedom to reach back to change the law. The restriction on retroactive legislation is strongest in criminal law through the bill of rights prohibition on *ex post facto* legislation. In other areas of the law, changing the rules after the fact gives unfair advantage to some parties and thus deprives others of contract rights or of property without due process.

Each legislature is also limited because it cannot deny to a later legislature the power to change the law for the future. Each new legislature starts with the full authority possessed by any of its predecessors. It may repeal, amend or extend any act of a past legislature, provided it does not give the change retroactive effect. This point is generally reduced to the truism: "No legislature can bind its successors." Few propositions of the law are so simple and yet so basic. In the legislative institution, the future always belongs to the future.

C. STRUCTURAL LIMITATIONS ON LEGISLATIVE POWER

§ 29–1. **Federal supremacy.** Article six of the United States Constitution provides:

This Constitution, and the laws of the United States which shall be made in pursuance thereof, and all treaties made, or which shall be made, under the authority of the United States, shall be the supreme law of the land, and the judges in every state shall be bound thereby, anything in the Constitution or laws of any state to the contrary notwithstanding.

This is the supremacy clause. It means a state legislature must always take into account policies adopted in Washington. When state action is in apparent conflict with federal law, two issues arise. The first is whether or not the congressional action falls within the powers granted to Congress. If Congress exceeded its authority, the action is invalid and, despite the supremacy clause, has no priority over state action. The second issue is whether or not Congress intended its policy to supercede state policy. Congress often acts without intent to pre-empt state policy making, or with an intent to pre-empt on a limited set of issues. It may be the congressional purpose that state and federal policies exist concurrently. The relative merit of the conflicting congressional and state legislative policies is not at issue. The congressional act may be extremely unwise compared to the state act, but a federal act and policy will control nonetheless if congressional intent is to pre-empt. Occasionally, when it acts on a problem, Congress provides explicitly that its action does not preclude state action in the area. This permits utilization of the states as testing grounds for alternative policies. Even

[*184*]

with such a provision, some degree of pre-emption may be unavoidable as the law is applied.

§ 29–2. **Separation of powers.** A fundamental principle of constitutional law is that one branch of government cannot exercise the powers of either of the other branches. In most state constitutions, the provision which grants legislative power to the legislature also grants judicial power to the judiciary and executive power to the executive. Coupled with separation of power are checks and balances that contemplate some interference by each of the branches with its coordinate branches. For example, the executive appoints judges and officials authorized by act of the legislature. He may veto legislation. By his budget proposals, he influences the legislative power of the purse. At the same time, the legislative appropriation power intrudes upon internal operations of the executive and judiciary. Senates hold power to reject executive appointments. Legislatures set salaries and they structure and restructure the other branches. Finally, the judiciary may set aside actions of the other branches which are substantively or procedurally unconstitutional.

The separation of powers doctrine in theory requires the legislature to do its own lawmaking. The legislature cannot delegate the job to administrative agencies or to the electorate through referenda on issues. The restriction on power to delegate shuts off some options for carrying out legislative work. The complexities of society have created a need for substantial delegation, however, and the doctrine against delegation is now tattered. Nonetheless, the doctrine has continuing significance which is discussed in § 38.

Another ramification of the separation of powers doctrine is denial of authority to the legislature to assume responsibilities which belong to the judiciary or the executive. For example, the power of appointment is an executive function. A legislature which creates an office and then fills it by legislative selection invades the prerogative of the executive. Therefore, the legislative appointment is invalid. For the legislature to assume a power of indictment, except in cases of impeachment, invades the power of the executive. The legislature cannot act as a judge of cases and controversies between parties based on past events, for adjudication of disputes is assigned to the judiciary.

§ 29–3. Federal courts versus state legislatures. The separation of powers principle contemplates checks and balances. Each branch holds some power over the others. However, the supremacy clause gives the branches of the federal government primacy over any branch of state government. This produces a serious breakdown in the theory of balanced power. When federal judges, enjoying lifetime tenure and independence from political pressure, take action which conflicts with policies set by state legislatures, the state legislature has no check or balance. The state holds little countervailing power and no power of retaliation.

The issue is not academic. In the last decade federal courts have exercised jurisdiction to set aside state policies on corrections, welfare, and the care of the institutionalized. Courts have ordered fundamental revision of spending priorities by declaring legislatively established programs in these areas illegal. Courts also repudiated policies for financing education which produced unequal tax burdens in different communities or unequal benefits for students in various localities. The federal courts in these cases set aside basic state policies and seem to be disarranging the allocation of responsibility in our system. However, courts will soon limit their intrusions to instances of gross legislative error or they will be crushed by the weight of petitioners unhappy with legislative decisions. A line of judicial restraint will be drawn to protect courts from countless lawsuits by the forces that now contend for appropriation priorities in the legislative arena.

The cases that cause federal courts to overturn legislative policy may be a consequence of inadequate lobbying at state legislatures. The stark misjudgments which give apparent validity to court incursions on state policy making ought not occur if citizens make presentations to legislatures as effectively as to courts. If the case is made to a legislature and does not prevail, other petitions may be even more persuasive. The courts have not faced the burden of balancing the competing requests for resource allocations that is so important a part of the legislative agenda. If they continue to invade legislative prerogatives by rewarding judicially those petitioners frustrated by legislative decisions, they soon will be deluged by plaintiffs asking the courts to overturn legislative policies, especially appropriation policies. If convicts, the mentally ill, the retarded, top female athletes, and students in poor districts receive federal court help to obtain an adequate share of state appropriations, are not mediocre athletes, average and gifted students, and the unemployed entitled to similar assistance?

D.   INITIATIVE AND REFERENDUM LIMITATIONS

§ 30–1. **Limitation on representative democracy.** Procedures of initiative and referendum compete with ordinary legislative procedure in a number of states. Initiative and referendum are separate devices, but so often occur in combination that their individual and distinct defects and claimed merits are seldom explained. Together or separate, they undermine the legislative institution and limit legislative power. Both grew out of the progressive movement of the early 20th century. The objective was to weaken, to bypass, and to reform corrupt legislatures. But weakening and reforming contradict one another. The high hopes of that progressive movement did not materialize and adoptions of initiative and referendum in recent decades have been rare.

Initiative and referendum were attacked at an early date as violating the clause of the federal constitution which mandates the republican form of government for each state. The legal challenge failed, but it revealed a flaw in the theory of initiative and referendum and helped slow the adoption of these approaches to direct democracy.

§ 30–2. **Referendum.** Referendum is the submission of a proposed law to the electorate for ratification. Four bases for submission exist: first, a constitution may provide for a ratification vote when some percent of the electorate petitions for it; second, the constitution may provide an automatic submission of specific kinds of legislation; third, initiated measures may go directly to a vote or may go on the ballot if the legislature does not ratify the initiated legislation; or fourth, the constitution may permit the legislature to ask for voter approval or rejection of its actions.

In all four variations, referendum gives legislators a means to pass the buck for policy making to the voters. In all variations, decision making turns into a public relations battle, rather than a process of deliberation. In all, the legislative institution is diminished. In all, the electorate faces extra and burdensome issue decisions in addition to choosing public officials from long lists of candidates.

A referendum is also part of the process of amending state constitutions. Amendments are submitted for voter ratification after legislative or convention endorsement. Many of the defects of referendum are present on a vote to change a constitution, but at least the voters are working on the fundamental government charter rather than ordinary legislation. Moods of the moment and political fads influence voter behavior less dramatically. Furthermore, voter approval of constitutional change maintains the consent-of-the-governed character of a constitution and no good substitute is available.

§ 30–3. **Initiative.** Initiative is a procedure which allows citizens to propose legislation by signing petitions. The draft legislation offered by the petitioners may go directly to voters for approval or may go first to the legislature and to the voters only if the legislature fails to act. The state constitution determines whether the issue is submitted directly or indirectly, or it may allow the petitioners to choose.

The essential role of words in legislation is overlooked by the initiative procedure. Zealous citizens who circulate initiative petitions rarely draft the law they propose carefully. Opportunity to correct errors is practically non-existent in initiative, in direct contrast to the refining and correcting of bills that dominates normal legislative processes. The opportunity to hear and accommodate dissenting views—to compromise—is slight. Initiative is not a liberal procedure, but a harsh method by which a majority may impose its will. It bypasses the moderating effect that examination by a deliberative, representative body has on legislation.

On major issues the legislature mirrors informed public opinion. In time, the public usually gets from legislatures what it sensibly demands. The political responsiveness of legislatures over the long term makes initiative and referendum unnecessary.

CHAPTER 9

THE STRUGGLE FOR LEGISLATIVE POWER

A. APPORTIONMENT

§ 31–1. **Effect of malapportionment.** As the decade of the 1960's began, the great power of legislatures was to a disproportionate degree held by rural America. Some country districts and districts in the commercial and industrial sections of central cities could appropriately be called rotten boroughs. A few hundred voters chose a legislator in these districts while the constituency of another legislator in a suburban community of the same state numbered hundreds of thousands of citizens. The malapportionment was reflected in Congress as well. In state after state the rural bias which arose from malapportionment produced legislatures which consciously favored rural constituents by putting small-population congressional districts into rural areas and large-population districts into urban areas. Malapportionment affected the substantive law produced by Congress and state legislatures. Outnumbered urban legislators could not force legislatures to give attention to urban problems. Those problems were swept under the rug.

§ 31–2. One man, one vote. In 1964 the United States Supreme Court held that state legislative districts must be drawn to provide equal representation to all citizens. Apportionments which failed to achieve this equality were declared defective and inoperative. Ultimately, where legislatures failed to apportion equitably, courts drew the district lines. The one man, one vote principle requirement was also extended to congressional districts.

The reapportionment decisions, capped by Reynolds v. Sims (377 U.S. 533), are probably the most significant in the court's history. If a transfer of power from one set of individuals to another is revolution, the years immediately following Reynolds v. Sims witnessed perhaps the greatest revolution in world history. In state after state, legislative power balances shifted from rural to urban constituencies. By the end of the decade, problems of urbanization were no longer pigeonholed, but were pushed onto legislative agendas. Once on the agenda, the problems received conscientious attention from all legislators, for the problems were then recognized as legitimate legislative concerns.

A short term by-product of one man, one vote was an improved quality in legislative members. Eliminating rotten boroughs forced pairs of incumbent legislators into single districts where the election rule was survival of the fittest. Metropolitan America benefited not only from additional representation of its own, but also from more competent and broader-minded rural legislators.

§ 31–3. Gerrymanders and other offenses.
Drawing boundaries for legislative and congressional districts offers opportunities for other inequities in addition to population imbalance. The gerrymander—drawing boundaries to concentrate or dissipate political strength—has a long history. If used to the detriment of a racial minority, the gerrymander will fall to judicial challenge. So far, the cases suggest judicial challenge is not likely to succeed when the motive for the gerrymander is simple partisan advantage. Concentrating or dissipating the voting strength of particular groups is most easily accomplished through the use of multi-member districts, rather than through gerrymanders. Where courts have drawn boundaries, they have used single-member districts. The courts have not yet invalidated a legislatively adopted plan because it used multi-member districts, but if evidence is presented showing a multi-member district discriminated against a racial minority, a challenge will likely succeed.

The struggle for legislative power through districting has been fought in both courts and legislatures. As the accumulation of judicial precedents made the ground rules for apportionment more definite, legislatures picked up the apportionment burden. Once equality was achieved, it was no longer an impossible task for the legislature itself to maintain fair representation. Consequently, the judicial role in apportionment is shrinking.

In some jurisdictions, legislatures have created outside groups to draw district lines. Districting is difficult for a legislative institution, since it sets party against party and colleague against colleague. Every member is directly affected by the provisions of an apportionment bill, so on this issue the usual division of labor does not work. Delegating the task of drawing district lines to non-legislative commissions has growing support because so much legislative energy is squandered in drafting and considering reapportionment bills.

B. ELECTION LAWS

§ 32–1. **Campaign practices.** Complicated and detailed statutes regulate the conduct of elections. These statutes set out regulations for the agencies which prepare ballots, arrange polling places, supervise voter registration, hire election judges, buy voting machines, and generally keep election machinery honest and efficient. The need for strict rules for the game of politics is obvious.

The portions of election laws that relate to campaign practices are the most pertinent to the struggle for legislative power. These *corrupt practice* or *fair campaign practices* acts define campaign sins and provide sanctions to be applied against those who transgress. Misrepresentations, anonymously produced pamphlets, and corporate contributions are practices commonly prohibited. Sanctions range from misdemeanor to felony penalties and, if the offender is the election winner, disqualification from office.

§ 32–2. New election regulations. Widespread efforts are under way to restructure and control the funding of political campaigns. The objectives are to equalize political opportunity and to reduce the distortions of public policy that result from conscious or subconscious *quid pro quo* attitudes between campaign contributors and elected officials. Public pressure to restrict campaign funding has crushed political resistance from entrenched interest groups. The greater obstacle to this legislation is the bill of rights. Almost any regulation of elections imposes direct restrictions on freedom of expression and direct and indirect restraint on free association and on privacy. If the conflict between these new election laws and the bill of rights cannot be avoided, election reform will have to take forms other than spending and contribution limits and disclosure of those

[*196*]

who contribute to campaigns. Another proposal in this area, public financing of campaigns, involves problems of equal protection, because any formula for distributing the funds will inevitably discriminate among candidates.

Campaign reform laws may simply give the illusion of reform. The burden is still on the voter, as it has been over the last two hundred years, to elect to office those with the character and the ability to act in the public interest.

C. LEGISLATOR ELECTION CHALLENGES

§ 33–1. House judge of own members. When an individual's election to a legislative body is challenged, the issue is judged by the house to which he seeks admission. The historical basis for this practice is parliament's need to insulate its members from the king and from the judges appointed by him. If the right to sit in parliament had been a judicial issue, the king's judges would have had power to exclude the king's adversaries from membership. To protect itself, parliament seized the power to admit or exclude its own members.

Election contests brought to the legislature involve the questions of who received the most votes and whether or not the election was conducted in accord with the fair campaign practices act of the jurisdiction. While legislatures may use other tribunals for preliminary fact-finding and even to recommend judgments, the ultimate decision rests with the legislative body. Given party and factional divisions, a legislature's judging of election contests is not above suspicion. Like redistricting, judging election contests can be carried on more efficiently and fairly outside the legislature. Unlike redistricting, the ancient prerogative of self-judgment has not been surrendered.

§ 33–2. Exceptions. The sovereignty of legislative bodies to judge their own membership was significantly qualified by the United States Supreme Court in 1966. In Bond v. Floyd (385 U.S. 116) the action of the Georgia House of Representatives excluding Julian Bond from its membership was reversed by the United States Supreme Court on the basis that the exclusion violated Bond's freedom of speech. Three years later in Powell v. McCormack (395 U.S. 486), the court ruled that Congress could exclude Adam Clayton Powell from membership only upon a finding that he failed to meet the constitutional qualifications for membership in the House of Representatives. Constitutional qualifications for office are very limited, usually including only age, residence, citizenship, and a willingness to take an oath to uphold the federal and state constitutions. The *Bond* and *Powell* cases add up to a rule that a legislative body may not violate an individual's right to a seat in the legislature nor his constituency's right to have him there unless the exclusion is based on his failure to meet the constitutional qualifications for the office or on defects in his election. The power to seat still rests entirely with legislatures. The *Bond* and *Powell* cases establish judicial review only when there is exclusion and then only if the exclusion is allegedly based upon unconstitutional foundations.

Legislative bodies have a separate power to expel from membership a member whose disorderly behavior or other misconduct makes his continued membership inappropriate. This power to expel is not conditioned upon qualifications. Whether it may be subject to free speech limitations, as is the right to exclude, has not been judicially tested. Expulsion normally requires an extraordinary vote comparable to the vote required to remove a judicial or executive officer through impeachment.

PART IV

LEGISLATURES AND COURTS

CHAPTER 10

CONSTITUTIONAL TESTS OF LEGISLATION

A. JUDICIAL POWER TO REVIEW

§ 34–1. Source and reason for the power. Courts and legislatures are coordinate, equal branches of government. Yet courts have assumed the power to declare legislative acts invalid. The power is not explicitly granted in the United States constitution nor in state constitutions. Whether courts possessed this power of review was in dispute until authoritatively established in Marbury v. Madison, (1 Cranch 137 (1804)). Justice Marshall's reasoning in *Marbury* (at 177) was:

> "It is, emphatically, the province and duty of the judicial department, to say what the law is. Those who apply the rule to particular cases, must of necessity expound and interpret that rule. If two laws conflict with each other, the courts must decide on the operation of each. So, if a law be in opposition

to the constitution; if both the law and the
constitution apply to a particular case, so
that the court must either decide that case,
conformable to the law, disregarding the constitution; or conformable to the constitution,
disregarding the law; the court must determine which of these conflicting rules governs
the case; this is of the very essence of judicial duty. If then, the courts are to regard
the constitution, and the constitution is superior to any ordinary act of the legislature,
the constitution, and not such ordinary act,
must govern the case to which they both apply."

In his masterpiece essay on constitutional law,
Judge Learned Hand commented on the import of
Marbury as follows:

For centuries it has been an accepted canon in interpretation of documents to interpo-
late into the text such provisions, though not
expressed, as are essential to prevent the defeat of the venture at hand; and this applies
with especial force to the interpretation of
constitutions, which, since they are designed
to cover a great multitude of necessarily un-
foreseen occasions, must be cast in general
language, unless they are constantly amended. If so, it was altogether in keeping with
established practice for the Supreme Court

to assume an authority to keep the states, Congress, and the President within their prescribed powers. Otherwise the government could not proceed as planned; and indeed would almost certainly have foundered, as in fact it almost did over that very issue. (The Bill of Rights, 1958, at 14–15).

§ 34–2. Judicial restraint. That a power first exercised by Chief Justice Marshall's court in 1804 and expounded in his most famous opinion still required Judge Hand to lend his mighty mind to its defense a century and half later reveals the sensitivity surrounding the issue of judicial review. Justice Brandeis in a concurring opinion in Ashwander v. TVA (56 S.Ct. 466 (1935)) observed that the court throughout its history "frequently called attention to the 'great gravity and delicacy' of its function in passing upon the validity of an act of Congress." Brandeis then listed the methods the court uses to restrain itself in the exercise of the power to overrule a decision of a coordinate branch. He included the following:

(a) The court will not pass on constitutionality in a non-adversary proceeding.

(b) The court will not anticipate a question of constitutional law in advance of the necessity of deciding it.

(c) The court will not formulate a rule of constitutional law broader than is required to decide the case before it.

(d) The court will not pass on a constitutional issue if there is present some other ground upon which the case may be disposed of.

(e) The court will if possible construe a statute to avoid the constitutional question.

(f) The court will not decide a constitutional question except upon the challenge of one injured by it.

(g) The court will not decide a constitutional challenge to a statute by one who has availed himself of its benefits.

§ 34–3. Presumption of constitutionality. Another restraint on the judicial review power is a presumption of constitutionality. Because of this presumption, those who challenge statutes must overcome strong intellectual, emotional, and political forces which incline a court against striking down a statute. The basis for the presumption is that a legislative decision to pass an act includes a determination that the act is valid; and that a court therefore puts itself in conflict with a conscious decision of the legislative branch if it finds an act unconstitutional. The case arrives at the court, in other words, not as a matter of first impression. The court has the last word, but the legislature has already made its decision.

The presumption of constitutionality also puts an act into effect. If a court later issues a decision ruling the act invalid, it changes the *status quo*. The conflict between the court and the legislature as a result appears more intense than it would without the presumption. Courts are disposed toward upholding statutes to avoid both conflict and the appearance of conflict.

§ 34–4.   **Severability.** When a court believes a statute is invalid and cannot avoid deciding the issue, it may still exercise restraint. It can escape direct conflict with at least some elements of the statute if it severs the invalid part and leaves the rest in effect. Appellate court opinions fail to reflect the full extent that severability rescues portions of statutes under attack. Parties fighting over one section ignore other parts of the statute; unless prompted by the litigators, courts forget to say that their decision does not affect the validity of those sections or applications of the act not relevant to the case. A court's opinion which implies that a statute is invalid in all respects and in all applications must be discounted; some of the act still may be effective. A lawyer attacking a statute can make it easier for a court to rule his way by limiting his challenge to that portion of the statute which damages his case, urging that the rest of the statute remain in effect.

§ 34–5. Effect of a declaration of invalidity.
Even though a court says a legislative act is invalid, the act remains on the statute books. A court cannot repeal legislation. In 1923 the United States Supreme Court declared all minimum wage laws unconstitutional; in 1937 the decision was overruled. This meant that the minimum wage law of the District of Columbia, dormant from 1923 to 1937, was suddenly in force as if newly adopted, even though it was seriously out of date. The reinterpretation of the constitution in 1937 by the Supreme Court eliminated the judgment of unconstitutionality so the statute was again in effect.

When one of its acts has been struck down, a legislature should be aware that the act has not been repealed, but only shelved in whole or in part. What should the legislature do? It may rewrite the act to repair whatever created the constitutional problem. If repair is impossible or inappropriate, it may repeal the act. It should not leave the act on the statute books as a trap for those who fail to note the impact of the decision holding the act invalid in whole or in part.

B. LEGISLATOR'S DUTY TO UPHOLD CONSTITUTION

§ 35–1. Oath of office. A state legislator begins his term of office with an oath to uphold the

constitutions of the United States and of his own
jurisdiction.   That is the only official promise he
makes.   The oath as regards the federal constitution is required by clause three of its sixth Article.   Drafters of state constitutions inserted similar provisions.   Constitution writers clearly intended to impose a responsibility for constitutional decision making on all officials, including legislators.   As legislators consider bills, however,
those without legal training, and some with law
degrees as well, feel inadequate to make decisions
on constitutionality.   Many are unwilling to face
up to constitutional issues.   This does not justify
relinquishing these questions to courts.   Judges
have no monopoly on the ability to read or to
think through the basic propositions contained in
a constitution.   In addition, legislators who hesi-
tate to make judgments on constitutional questions regularly make other decisions for which
they have as little training, experience, or information.

§ 35–2.   **Practical reasons.**   For two practical
reasons, legislators cannot renege on their oath to
uphold the constitution and the resulting obligation to make decisions on constitutionality.
First, the judicial presumption of constitutionality is based on the belief that the legislature
has done its share of the job.   Courts are reluctant to hold an act unconstitutional because they

assume that decision contradicts a prior, thoughtful decision by a coordinate branch. If legislatures shirk this responsibility, the presumption has no factual basis. The law usually disposes of legal presumptions which are baseless, so legislators, if they value this presumption as they should, must protect it by fulfilling their obligation.

Second, when a legislature passes a law, the community presumes it is constitutional. People act because of its provisions in ways they would not act if it had not been passed. Those adversely affected by the law must either suffer its effects or bring a lawsuit to present the issue to a court. If a legislator believes a bill is unconstitutional, but casts a vote to pass it anyway, the vote imposes unfair burdens. Litigation is expensive in time, money, and energy. A legislator does injustice by making any citizen choose either to sue or to suffer.

A realistic examination of legislative performance on constitutional issues must include political considerations. If public opinion runs strong, and especially if the issue is close, political expediency may cause a legislator to vote for a bill even if he believes it is invalid. That this happens does not mean it is justified.

In one circumstance, a legislator can legitimately vote for a bill he thinks a court will declare unconstitutional. That circumstance occurs when he believes the court to be wrong and his own interpretation to be consistent with the meaning intended by the writers and ratifiers of the constitution.

C.   MAJOR FOUNDATIONS FOR CONSTITUTIONAL CHALLENGE

§ 36–1.   **Constitutional pegs.**   A constitutional challenge to legislation must be based on some specific provision; there must be a peg on which to hang the attack.   A few towering propositions underlie most constitutional assaults on legislation.   Procedural due process of law, equal protection, and the fundamental freedoms of the first amendment—the basic, giant, ever-expanding principles of constitutional law—encompass such dynamic values in our legal system that they dominate judicial review.   These are discussed in the next few sections, as is the controversial doc-trine of substantive due process.

§ 36–2.   **Procedural due process.**   Due process undergirds judicial review of any legislation which establishes legal procedure.   A court may find unconstitutional procedures in the whole thrust of a legislative act or in its application to a specific situation.   In either case a ruling of un-constitutionality forces the legislature to repair the act.   Among the main elements of procedural due process are reasonable notice, an opportunity to be heard and to present evidence, and a fair tribunal. In criminal cases, procedural rights also include representation by counsel, speedy and public trial, confrontation of witnesses, and jury trial. Bills must provide the essentials of due process, either in the bill or in its statutory and real life context. Incorporation by reference of another statute which has already been tested is particularly useful to avoid due process defects.

§ 36–3. **Substantive due process.** Legislation is also subjected to due process review in its substantive aspects. Economic substantive due process was the judicial weapon used against the New Deal in the 1930's and against earlier legislative efforts to regulate business. Economic substantive due process originated with Allgeyer v. Louisiana (17 S.Ct. 427 (1897)) which held that state legislative restrictions on foreign insurance companies infringed "the liberty of contract." Over a number of decades the courts aggressively protected business from legislative regulation. For example, in 1905 laws setting maximum hours for work were held invalid; and in 1923 the court held that both federal and state legislation setting minimum wages deprived business of liberty without due process of law. The court also used substantive due process to overrule state legislation on yellow dog contracts, price fixing, and arbitration of wage disputes. Economic substantive due process was overturned by a 5 to 4 decision in West Coast Hotel Co. v. Parrish (57 S.Ct. 578 (1937)) and has been shunned by the Supreme Court since then.   Commentators now recognize that courts had set themselves up as super legislatures and appropriately condemn the theoretical base for that judicial domination.

Substantive due process may be making a comeback, but not in its economic liberty aspects. The abortion and birth control decisions, based on substantive rights of privacy or self-determination, are viewed by some commentators as substantive due process decisions.   Privacy has been labeled a liberty which cannot be taken without due process of law, just as freedom to contract was so labeled in *Allgeyer*.   Cases have also held that incarceration and mental commitments not followed by minimally adequate treatment or by efforts at rehabilitation deprive convicts and mental patients of due process.   The difference from the old substantive due process is that the court now is protecting personal liberty, not economic liberty.   Today legislation which clashes with individual rights is suspect, whereas legislation regulating the economic affairs of the community is not.   Judicial second guessing of legislative policy involving economic judgments earned such a bad reputation in the first four decades of the 20th century that it is not likely to be revived in the foreseeable future.   But a new substantive due process protection of individual rights regarding care and treatment, privacy, travel, religion, speech, press, assembly, association and self-determination has become a significant judicial check on legislative policy.

§ 36–4. Equal protection.   The requirement that everyone be accorded equal protection of the law parallels due process—and rivals it in significance.   This provision of the constitution provided the basis for the school desegregation cases, the reapportionment cases, the equality of educational opportunity and tax burden cases, and the non-resident tuition and welfare rights cases. Legislatures always draw boundary lines in legislation—some persons are included and some excluded.   The boundary lines between included and excluded classes are subject to equal protection examination.   Equal protection at the moment receives in the Supreme Court a two-tier analysis based on whether the challenged classification is suspect or not.   Suspect classifications are race, religion, residence, economic status, and perhaps sex.   If the classification is suspect, the statute is given strict scrutiny and only a powerful reason can overcome the presumption of invalidity.   If a suspect classification is not involved, the statute is given a more sympathetic reading and is upheld if there is a rational basis for the classification, considering the purpose of the statute.

Justice Thurgood Marshall has found the two-tier analysis unsatisfactory. He has said it is unrealistic to insist on a dichotomy when what actually exists is a spectrum of suspiciousness, not two tiers. On the other part of the two-tier process, Marshall has a similar problem. Legislative justification for classifications do not fall neatly in or out of something identifiable as a rational basis; justifications for distinctions also range on a spectrum. In action, though not in words, the court is clearly moving toward the Marshall approach of subjectively balancing the inequities of a legislative classification against the policy justification for the classes established.

§ 36–5.   Preferred freedoms.   When the actual law or an official administering the law cuts into one of the liberties that courts embrace with special foundness, the flag goes up and the act is in legal trouble. These preferred freedoms involve travel, privacy, religion, speech, press, assembly, and association. The policy clashes between court and legislature (between constitution and statute) occur frequently on these questions. Passing an act that infringes on one of these freedoms is not a problem of legislative motive as much as inability to imagine in advance the way legislation will affect specific circumstances. Harsh consequences to individuals are lost from view in the search for the "greatest good for the greatest number" during legislative deliberations. Legislatures are not without sin, of course. Thomas Jefferson and his allies insisted on the first ten amendments to the constitution, the Bill of Rights, with the knowledge that government —even republican government—would on occasion push individual citizens around. Legislatures, responsive to majority pressure or to pressure from intense minorities, at times forget the fundamental rights of individuals.

§ 36–6. Ebb and flow of preferred pegs. Legal history shows an ebb and flow in the impact of constitutional provisions. At various times the changing personnel of the court finds different principles more congenial to its way of thinking. Justice Jackson, in 1947, persuasively endorsed equal protection as a judicial rein on legislative action to substitute for the rein of substantive due process. Jackson said:

> "The burden should rest heavily upon one who would persuade us to use the due process clause to strike down a substantive law or ordinance. Even its provident use against municipal regulations frequently disables all government—state, municipal and federal— from dealing with the conduct in question because the requirement of due process is also applicable to State and Federal Governments. Invalidation of a statute or an ordi-

nance on due process grounds leaves ungoverned and ungovernable conduct which many people find objectionable.

Invocation of the equal protection clause, on the other hand, does not disable any governmental body from dealing with the subject at hand. It merely means that the prohibition or regulation must have a broader impact. I regard it as a salutary doctrine that cities, states and the Federal Government must exercise their powers so as not to discriminate between their inhabitants except upon some reasonable differentiation fairly related to the object of regulation. This equality is not merely abstract justice. The framers of the Constitution knew, and we should not forget today, that there is no more effective practical guaranty against arbitrary and unreasonable government than to require that the principles of law which officials would impose upon a minority must be imposed generally. Conversely, nothing opens the door to arbitrary action so effectively as to allow those officials to pick and choose only a few to whom they will apply legislation and thus to escape the political retribution that might be vested upon them if larger numbers were affected. Courts can take no better measure to assure that laws

[214]

will be just than to require that laws be equal in operation." (Railway Express v. New York, 69 S.Ct. 463 at 466 (1949)).

Justice Jackson's opinion displays great respect for legislative prerogatives and an understanding of the need to avoid, if possible, conclusive confrontations between court and legislature. He suggested a variety of judicial restraint that uses a review which says: "You cannot do it *that* way" rather than "You cannot do it at all." A few years later Jackson's preferred judicial tool of equal protection shaped many of the powerful public policy decisions of the Warren court. The old economic due process doctrine was not revived by the activist Warren court, but legislative policy was, nonetheless subjected to meaningful review under the equal protection clause. Other review of legislative action by the Warren court was consistent with Jackson's preference for review of means rather than ends. The Warren court used procedural due process review more than the court had at any earlier time. The procedural emphasis still prevails. It is so strong, in fact, that some writers contend it verges on substantive review. In a recent example, the Burger court held that the absence of any procedure to overcome factual presumptions on residence invalidated distinctions between residents and nonresidents. Some scholars believe the clause offended against was the equal protection clause, rather than the due process clause. This residency case demonstrates how one clause overlaps others and how, in the review of legislation, they may be combined to produce something more far-reaching than any clause standing alone.

CHAPTER 11

TECHNICALITIES AFFECTING SUBSTANCE

A. RETROACTIVITY

§ 37–1. Unfairness. When a legislature changes the law after the fact, it is usually acting unfairly and unconstitutionally. Retroactive legislation deprives someone of the benefit of vested legal rights without due process of law. If a contract right is lost, the change violates the constitutional provision against abridging the obligation of contract and the due process clause. The doctrine prohibiting retroactive legislation is built on these two constitutional clauses.

Constitutional principles aside, it would be disastrous to allow legislatures to decide legal disputes by changing rules to suit petitioners. Both the sense and reality of justice would be shattered if private affairs were decided in the political arena with new rules established for old facts. Legislators know this; the rule against retroactivity is rarely questioned by legislators who are aware of it and is usually followed instinctively by legislators who never receive a formal explanation of the principle.

§ 37–2. Curative acts. Legislatures may pass valid retroactive legislation in circumstances where it is fair to do so. Any act intended to reach back in time to correct errors of the past must be clearly drafted to indicate the retroactive intention, for there is a strong presumption that legislation is intended to have only prospective effect. Since the prohibition on retroactivity is based on its unfairness, the bar does not apply if fairness and justice are served by giving an act retroactive effect. Acts to cure defects in the law or to correct procedural errors are called curative. If a curative act is attacked on the basis of its retroactivity, its validity depends somewhat on whether the challenger relied on the former law. Reliance and change of position based on the old law does not make curative legislation automatically invalid. The test is justice. The usual presumption of constitutionality applies to curative acts; legislative conduct with curative acts is cautious enough to support the presumption.

§ 37–3. Procedural — substantive distinction. When an event occurs, its legal consequences are decided by the law then in effect. The rights of the parties are not vulnerable to subsequent modification of the law. The method by which the vested rights of the parties to the event are adjudicated may be changed, however. If a legislature or court fashions a new mechanism to more efficiently and fairly adjudicate disputes, pre-existing disputes ought to be determined under the new and better procedure. In short, the rule against retroactivity applies to the substantive law, not to procedural law. It is often said that procedural law can be changed retroactively, but this is inaccurate. What is meant is that newly adopted procedural rules may be used for old conflicts. A procedural change, in a literal sense, can never be retroactive, since a new procedure can never be used yesterday.

§ 37–4. Ex post facto criminal laws. Retroactive changes in criminal law are barred as *ex post facto* laws (after the fact laws). The prohibition of *ex post facto* laws applies to all changes detrimental to the defendant, whether in procedure, in the substantive elements of a crime, or in the punishments which may be imposed after conviction. The procedural-substantive distinction explained in the previous section is modified in criminal prosecutions. Usually, the defendant has a vested right in any procedure which benefits him. Since the state is a party to the prosecution and also makes the procedural rules, it is prohibited from changing those rules to the detriment of a defendant.

§ 37–5. Bills of attainder. Bills of attainder are legislative acts which: (1) punish (2) specified persons (3) without a judicial proceeding. The prohibition on bills of attainder is based partly on the problem of retroactivity and partly on separation of powers. The separation of powers element is that the legislature does not hold power to act as judge of cases. The retroactive element is that a legislature cannot impose sanctions upon past behavior. Close questions arise as to whether an act is a bill of attainder if it limits those who may enjoy some right or privilege. If those disqualified are few in number and the basis for disqualification is past activity, the bill may slip over into the bill of attainder class. For example, in U. S. v. Brown (85 S.Ct. 1707 (1965)) the court held a congressional act which barred persons who had been members of the Communist party from labor union office was invalid as a bill of attainder.

B.   DELEGATION OF POWER

§ 38–1.   **Traditional rules on delegation.**   Discussion of legislative power to delegate responsibility to others—and the limitations on that power—requires walking a tightrope between what courts say and what they do. Legal theory on delegation is unsatisfactory, so judicial action is unreliable. Courts long ago constructed an elaborate body of law restricting the power to delegate; without expressly tearing it down, they have ignored it for years. The problems and evils of delegation are severe enough so that the current anarchy in the field is not likely to continue. Also some basic portions of the early body of law continue to be applied, partly as form and partly as substance.

The law started with the proposition that legislative power had to be exercised by the legislature, not delegated to others. Legislatures responded with more and more delegation, which led the courts to surrender—almost. The next generation of cases said the legislature must lay down standards to control the use of whatever power was delegated. Legislatures responded by stating standards like: just and reasonable, for the general welfare, to prevent unfair competition. The courts surrendered again; today they accept these meaningless phrases as adequate standards.

The reasons for the original prohibition on delegation and for requiring standards are still valid. First, legislators must be accountable for public policy, but delegation to administrative agencies or subordinate units of government interferes with that accountability. Second, the law must be accessible to citizens, but legislation enacted without detail or standards produces law hidden in the labyrinth of informal agency behavior. This law is not published or even written down.

§ 38–2. Professor Davis' suggestion. Professor Kenneth Culp Davis proposes a response to the conflicting currents around the delegation doctrine. In *Discretionary Justice* (Tulane Press, 1971) Davis developed this view of delegation: legislatures will delegate, courts will allow delegation, agencies will accept delegated power and exercise it arbitrarily unless checked in some way, courts and legislatures and executives do not now check agencies, and something new is needed to deal with the problem. Davis offers this resolution: let legislatures delegate, insist on meaningful standards for the exercise of delegated power but permit the standards to be spelled out over a period of time by the agency to which the delegation is made, further require the agency to record and maintain as open precedents the facts found and the rules applied in its cases, require the agency to explain deviations from its established precedents, require the agency from time to time to codify in general rules its accumulated precedents, and allow a party to defeat an agency action by showing in court that the agency is not keeping its rules up to date or not maintaining and following its established precedents.

The attractiveness of the Davis proposal is that it does not expect the impossible from the institutions of government. Legislatures are permitted to use administrative agencies in the rough way they are inclined to; that is, the agency is sent out into the real world to slay the dragon, even though the legislature does not know how to do it. Davis' proposal gives a court some materials with which to review the work of an agency. These materials are agency precedents including explanations, agency rules, and the record in the specific case under review. The court, with these materials, need not defer blindly to agency expertise. The court can force an agency to lay out its policies for the public to follow or to challenge. The legislature can also better oversee agency performance by examining the agency's precedents and regulations. When the legislature knows agency policy it has the ability to dissent, for it may pass an act imposing a different policy. Under current practice much agency policy is hidden from everyone—courts, legislature, public, and the agency itself.

Whether the Davis proposal will be accepted, either extensively or in a limited way, is uncertain. What is certain is that there will be agency resistance to it. The proposal is intended to limit agency power, and it does so by imposing new chores on agencies. Bureaucrats will protest; they will also claim great new costs in an effort to defeat any legislation imposing the Davis theory. Courts, however, can adopt his approach to judicial review of agency actions without legislative action.

§ 38–3. Incorporation by reference. The useful drafting technique of including other documents in a bill by reference occasionally runs afoul of the non-delegation doctrine. The problem occurs when future change in the incorporated material is included. This gives those who can change the incorporated material the power to change the legislation. If future changes in federal income taxes are incorporated in a state income tax law, the legislature is delegating to Congress the power to amend state tax law. This is prohibited. If future changes in the National Electrical Code are incorporated into a state's statutes, power to make the law is delegated to the America Standards Institute which writes that code. This is prohibited. The prohibition does not bar incorporation of any edition of the National Electrical Code published prior to the incorporation. Congressional acts, not including future amendments, may also be incorporated by reference. But the legislature cannot give a blank check to another institution to change the law of the state.

This does not prevent other institutions from holding power over a state's law. For example, most states have soldiers and sailors acts which are in effect when Congress has declared a state of war. This qualification is not a delegation but a condition depending on a fact of independent significance. It just happens that Congress controls that fact.

Non-delegation does not bar incorporation of other acts of the same legislature—including future amendments. Since amendments come from the same institution, power is not surrendered to others. Incorporation of other statutes is an immensely valuable drafting strategy. It permits the draftsman to borrow for his bill provisions which have already been legislatively examined. The policy judgments represented in the incorporated sections therefore are not reexamined closely by the legislature. Incorporation makes a bill shorter, which means there is less to explain. It is less intimidating.

There are negative aspects to incorporation. Incorporated language is not reexamined, which means any defect continues on with a double impact. The imperfection might have been corrected had it been copied and put into the new bill verbatim rather than by incorporation. Also the extent of incorporation may be obscure. One statute may not fit perfectly into another, yet incorporation assumes it does. Serious ambiguity results from misfit incorporations; therefore the effect of inserting provisions into a law for which they were not drawn must be examined. The new bill must indicate clearly whether future amendments to the old statute are included in the incorporation. Generally they are included, under the provisions of the state's statutory construction act.

§ 38–4. Voter referenda prohibited. The nondelegation doctrine extends to the electorate as well as to agencies. Except in the twenty-five jurisdictions which by constitution authorize submission of legislation to the electorate for ratification, legislatures cannot pass responsibility for lawmaking to the voters. Even where such action is invalid, the suggestion surfaces when an issue is controversial because politically it appeals to many legislators to "let the people decide."

C. TITLE AND DOUBLE SUBJECT

§ 39–1. Double subject. A common provision of state constitutions is: "Each bill shall have a single subject which shall be expressed in its title." This provision prevents throwing separate provisions together in an arbitrary way. It imposes an external discipline on the legislative process. Congress is under no such constitutional restraint, although the rules of house and senate attempt to limit disparate provisions in bills. Combining ideas in one bill to accumulate support that the ideas could not win separately precludes a decision on the merits. Each provision moves to passage under the protective cover of the others.

The double-subject prohibition is stronger in theory than in reality.   Courts have tolerated this legislative practice for they appreciate the necessity to combine legislative business into packages.   There is no possibility that each separate legislative idea can be a separate bill.   The waste and confusion would be monumental if that were tried.   What courts have demanded—sporadically—is an effort at reasonably honest packaging.   They have required that the multiple objectives of a bill not be discordant.   If a common element links its provisions, the bill is upheld.   A bill for the enactment of revised laws (a reenactment of all the statutory law of the state) has a single subject.   The enactment of a three hundred page bill significantly modifying all the commercial law of a state (the Uniform Commercial Code) is upheld, since there is a unity of subject within its broad reach.   Courts are less tolerant if they detect a union of private interests within a bill.   Special interest legislation gets a more suspicious double-subject examination, for a merger of self-seeking petitioners is the evil at which the double-subject rule is primarily aimed.

§ 39–2.   **Title.**   The title requirement has its separate purpose, but is irrevocably wedded to the double-subject prohibition.   By simple craftsmanship, the writer of a bill can cure a double-subject problem when he drafts a title which covers everything in the bill and shows a unity in its provisions. Some unifying factor can almost invariably be found. In addition, a title which states a single subject, but fails to cover the entire contents of the bill, provides a way for a court to cure a double-subject defect. Parts of the bill not reflected in the title can be severed by the court as invalid under the title requirement. Then the rest of the bill has a single subject and can be upheld.

The purpose of a title is to give to the public and legislature notice of the contents of the bill. The test of a valid title is honesty, rather than completeness. The most terse title is legally adequate, even one simply listing the number of a statute amended by the bill. Only if the title misleads the reader about the contents of the bill are portions vulnerable to attack. Well-drafted bills adhere to more stringent standards than those imposed by courts. Legislators like helpful titles. Also a candid, comprehensible title wins votes, for it suggests the bill has the same characteristics. Requirements and styles vary somewhat from state to state, but the following guides for bill drafters are appropriate to most jurisdictions:

(a) State a single subject before using a conjunction, otherwise the title suggests a double subject.

(b) After stating a single general subject, list the main provisions of the bill, not omitting any provision with as much significance as those mentioned. These provisions ought to honestly alert the reader to the substance of the bill.

(c) Say "providing penalties" if criminal provisions are included.

(d) Enumerate all prior legislation which is amended by the bill.

(e) Enumerate all prior legislation which is repealed by the bill.

D. SPECIAL LEGISLATION

§ 40–1. Evils of special legislation. Special legislation is prohibited by most state constitutions, but it is passed nonetheless. The prohibition is included because special legislation uses up legislative energy in bits and pieces, leaving the institution handicapped in its ability to deal with general legislative business. Fortunately, procedural shortcuts, primarily consent calendars for noncontroversial bills, keep the actual effort far below that which is assumed by observers who merely count the number of special bills introduced or passed. Procedural shortcuts sometimes result in ill-considered policy decisions, however. If a bill applies to a single unit of government and has the support of the governing body of that unit, the legislature gives the bill superficial attention; policy may be adopted which would never be approved if the issue were examined for statewide application. As a consequence, the legislature fails to establish responsible and uniform statewide regulation of local governmental units and creates through special acts preferential and prejudicial discrimination between communities.

Another evil of special legislation is that legislators use the opportunity to pass local legislation for personal political and economic advantage in their home communities. Since a legislator's local bills generally are passed routinely, this opportunity is subject to arbitrary use. Legislators who control local bill committees may also be tempted to an abuse of power. They may use those bills as hostages to obtain votes on other issues. This destructive tactic works with weak legislators, since it is difficult and embarrassing for the timid officeholder to explain why a local bill desired by some constituents did not pass when similar bills were passed for other communities. Strong legislators call the bluff, so the technique does not do as much harm as it could.

Two controls on local special bills exist that are more effective than constitutional prohibition. One is a critical attitude toward special legislation in the legislature. The other is a base of general legislation which provides adequate powers and regulation for local units on a statewide basis. With good general law, a presumption arises within the legislature that communities do not need special treatment. Local bills become difficult to pass, so legislators are more likely to tackle problems on a general, statewide basis.

§ 40–2. **Bogus general legislation.** The prohibition on special legislation often is stated in a constitution as a provision barring a special act where a general law could apply. Such a provision is meaningless because any rule can be drawn to apply statewide if common sense and the purpose of the rule are ignored. The provision also is impractical, because it interferes with special legislative treatment of special problems.

The prohibition has been evaded by cloaking special laws in the garb of general legislation. A special bill for one local unit is drawn to apply to all units meeting specific criteria. The criteria actually limit its applicability to the one community the sponsors intend to affect. Population is the most common criterion since it is handy to use. Courts defer to the legislature by upholding these spurious classifications mainly because courts have not developed general rules which separate unnecessary special acts from those which are useful.

Using artificial, general-law classifications to camouflage local legislation creates two special problems. First, it may not be obvious which community is affected. Those who do not have the identifying codes do not know that a law for a county of "X population and Y area" applies to *Able* county and no other. The target county is semi-secret. Second, at the next census *Able* county may change population and no longer fit the description; and some other county which wants nothing to do with the legislation may fall into the class. Until the codes based on population are changed in the old acts, local governments take actions without legislative authority. Curative acts may be necessary, but may create due process problems.

The vulnerability to shifting application of special legislation as population changes is a result of the judicial requirement that classifications must be open. *Open* means other units must come under the law if they meet the criteria in the law. This is necessary to protect the charade that the act is general legislation. If the class is fixed by the facts at some point in time, it is *closed*. The class then is stripped of any presumption that it is an honest classification related to the legislation purpose. Instead it is held to be descriptive of the target community. As such, it is an invalid special law.

CHAPTER 12

JUDICIAL SUPERVISION OF LEGISLATIVE PROCEDURE

A. ENROLLED BILL RULE VERSUS JOURNAL ENTRY RULE

§ 41–1. **Enrolled bill rule.** At the end of the legislative process an official bill document is filed in the office of the secretary of state. It bears the signatures of the officers of each house certifying action on the measure by their respective bodies. It also carries the signature of the executive, indicating his approval, or appropriate documentation of an override of his veto. This document is the enrolled act. Under federal cases and judicial decisions in somewhat less than half the states, the enrolled bill is conclusively presumed to have been validly adopted. Judicial inquiry into legislative procedure is barred as an intrusion into the internal affairs of the legislature. This is the enrolled bill rule. It is based in part on the fact that judicial review of whether or not the legislature followed constitutional mandates in processing legislation does not possess the same claim to legitimacy as substantive judicial review. First, the court does not have greater ability to judge procedural legitimacy, since constitutional rules on procedure are easily mas-

tered.   Procedural disputes are over facts—
whether or not the bill had enough votes, or
three readings, or whatever—not over the meaning of the constitution.   Legislators, as eyewit-
nesses, are in a better position than the court to
rule on the facts.

The argument is also made that if a court can
go behind an enrolled bill to check on procedure,
the legislature can with as much justification go
behind a final judgment of a court.   The assump-
tion is that legislatures are offended if a court examines legislative procedure.

An additional rationale for the enrolled bill rule
is that it gives stability to the law.   Citizens reasonably assume that filed acts are valid.   To void
an act on procedural grounds traps those who in
good faith relied on the legislation.   Many courts
hold that legislation must "carry its death war-
rant in its hand" (that is, on its face) before a
court can invalidate it.   Defects of due process,
equal protection, free speech, double subject, title,
special legislation, delegation and other defects of
legislative content and style appear on the face of
legislation and therefore are easily discernible.
They do not deserve or receive the immunity
from judicial assault granted to transgressions of
legislative procedure.

§ 41–2.   Journal entry rule.   Under the journal
entry rule, which is followed in a majority of ju-

risdictions, a court may go behind the enrolled bill to the official journals of the legislature to determine if constitutional mandates on procedure were met. Stability of law is protected under the journal entry rule by the fact that inquiry is not permitted beyond journal entries and by a presumption that every procedural requirement was met unless the journal affirmatively shows otherwise. In one appellate case, the *aye* and *nay* votes recorded in the journal showed the absence of a two-thirds vote on a motion for which that margin was constitutionally required, yet a court asserted that the journal entries did not establish that the same motion was not put at another time, carried with sufficient votes, and omitted from the journal by oversight. The court excused the journal defect because the bill received better than a two-thirds vote on final passage.

The rationale for the journal entry rule is necessity. If a court cannot enforce a constitution's procedural orders, the legislature can ignore those mandates with impunity. A procedural check offends legislatures no more than a check on the substance of legislation. In reality, to have a court overturn an act because of a procedural defect bothers legislators less than to have legislation overturned on substantive grounds. The procedural check protects legislative minorities and the institution itself from abuse of its rules. The court reinforces legislative self-discipline by providing an outside procedural check. Most significantly a procedural error which makes legislation invalid can be corrected by repassage of the bill. But if legislation is struck down on substantive grounds, judicial policy may be permanently substituted for legislative policy; the judges' substantive interpretation of the constitution becomes a bar to further legislative action. The legislature is permanently blocked from its policy choice.

§ 41–3. Limited effect of journal entry rule. The judiciary imposes strict restraints on its review of legislative procedure even where the journal entry rule prevails. It is so hard to overcome the presumptions favoring validity of an act that the difference between the enrolled bill rule and the journal entry rule barely justifies the intellectual energy that has been devoted to examining the distinction. To stop the examination of legislative procedure at the official record maintained by the legislature means there is no judicial review of any violation willfully concealed by false entries in the journal. A case can be made for review of procedure which looks at the facts, rather than stopping at journal entries. For example, legislatures with fixed adjournment dates sometimes continue the journal of the last legal day for a number of days thereafter. Everyone who reads news reports, including the judges of the state, are aware the constitution is being evaded. However, the journal entry rule proscribes subsequent attack upon acts passed after the deadline because the journal shows action on an earlier, legal date.

The journal entry rule is a convenient and effective compromise between unlimited oversight of procedure and no oversight at all. A legislature is reluctant to falsify its official record, so review of the journal does reveal most procedural defects. When the journal is written to misrepresent the facts, it is usually done with unanimous consent because the constitutional provision violated is unrealistic. Constitutions are living documents and a legislature must sometimes adjust procedural provisions to get its job done, just as courts do.

B. JOURNAL ENTRY RULE APPLIED

§ 42–1. **Defects subject to journal entry review.** State constitutions impose a variety of procedural requirements and prohibitions. In a jurisdiction which has the journal entry rule, the following legislative procedures are typically subject to judicial review:

(a) Non-identical bills. Assembly and senate must pass a bill and the executive must sign it to make it a valid act. Each must put its official

imprimatur on a single document. If a review of
the journal discloses any variation in the text acted on by any one of the three, a court will declare
the legislation invalid. Under the enrolled bill
rule, on the other hand, the document signed and
delivered to the secretary of state by the governor is conclusively presumed to be the version
passed by assembly and senate.

(b) *Ayes* and *nays* recorded. Many state constitutions require that the *ayes* and *nays* be recorded on final passage votes. If sufficient
names are not recorded in the *yes* column in the
journal, the act is subject to successful challenge.
The Congress is not under this mandate and passes most bills by voice vote, often by only a handful of members. In Congress, as in all state legislatures, votes on final passage must be recorded if
any member demands a roll call.

(c) Sufficient affirmative votes. Recording
names on final passage or recording the number
of votes for or against are ways to meet the common constitutional requirement that some minimum number of affirmative votes be cast for a
measure. A minimum vote requirement is usually a majority of all members elected. Some bills
—usually those to authorize capital expenditures,
borrowing, special taxes, or to propose constitutional amendments—require more votes. The
journal entry may be examined to confirm that
the bill received sufficient votes. A South Dako-

ta case held that where a bill contained some appropriation items requiring a two-thirds vote and other items requiring a simple majority, the latter were valid and the former were severed as invalid because the recorded vote fell between a majority and two thirds.

(d) Three readings. A common requirement is that a bill receive three readings, each on a separate day. The journal entry may be examined to see if the mandate was met or if some emergency loophole was properly utilized. When the requirement is that any of the readings be at length, journals falsely imply that at-length readings occur. Since courts do not inquire into the reality behind the journal, this pretense works in most jurisdictions. But in a few states, courts have locked themselves into historical anomalies, and the legislature is forced to hire a chorus of readers to chant the words of pending legislation when the chamber is not being used for the real work of the legislature. No sensible court should force this charade on its legislature. The need for oral reading ended when most legislators became literate.

(e) Revenue bills from assembly. Following the pattern of the federal constitution, state constitutions usually require tax-raising bills to originate in the lower house. This means simply that an act for taxation must pass the assembly first. It is of no consequence what amendments the

senate adds.   Occasionally this mandate, usually
insignificant, snares a piece of legislation by accident.   This occurs when the tax aspect is inciden-
tal to the larger purpose and consequently overlooked, for example with a building program to
be financed by state bonds.   Unless the tax authorization underlying the bonds is spotted, a senate rather than an assembly bill may be processed and turn up in the office of the secretary of
state.   If challenged, the bill is subject to invali-
dation in its entirety or in its tax aspects.

§ 42–2.   **No review of rules violations.**   Each
legislative body adopts rules to make its procedures regular and fair.   These rules protect minorities from arbitrary action.   A two-thirds vote may
usually suspend a rule which impedes action desired by that extraordinary majority, but fewer than
that cannot excuse the body from its self-imposed
mandates.   However, even if a body's journal
shows breach of its rules, courts cannot invalidate
an act on that ground.   The violation, by custom,
is treated as a suspension of the rule, since the
majority which ignored the rule could have
amended the rule if it decided to do so.   The only
rules judicially enforced are those mandated by
the constitution, because a court may interfere
with the internal procedures of its coordinate
branch only to uphold the constitution.

CHAPTER 13

STATUTORY INTERPRETATION

A. PRINCIPLES OF STATUTORY INTERPRETATION

§ 43–1. **Legislative imperfection.** Accepting with sympathetic understanding the fallibility of legislative institutions—often comical fallibility —puts the task of statutory interpretation into proper perspective. The statutes of a legislature do not emerge like a Eugene O'Neill drama, as the product of months of work by a brilliant mind, polished by rewriting during weeks of rehearsal and out-of-town tryouts. A legislative act emerges from the hubbub of legislative struggle, from the drafts of beginning lawyers, from the work of lobbyists casual about clarity but forceful about policy, and from the chaos of adjournment deadlines. A legislative act comes from committee effort, one more reason to expect the message to be a bit self-contradictory. Committees rarely speak with a single thought, with a totally consistent objective. Eugene O'Neill dramas confuse; so do statutes. No one should be surprised.

§ 43–2. **Who interprets statutes.** Anyone who opens a statute book and attempts to puzzle out the meaning of the law is engaged in statutory interpretation (often called statutory construction). The most authoritative statutory interpretation occurs in appellate courts. When the meaning of a legislative act is at issue, the appellate court opinion discusses the provision and explains the reasons for giving it whatever meaning is settled upon by the panel. The law then becomes the statutory words as modified by the judicial interpretation of them. Over the years, a set of standardized rules that courts and others use in statutory interpretation has evolved from appellate court explanations of how they arrive at the meaning of statutes presented to them in litigation. These rules are called canons of statutory interpretation.

Only a small percentage of all statutory language is ever subjected to appellate court scrutiny. This means the greater part of interpretation occurs independent of appellate litigation. Running downward in authoritativeness and upward in the number of decisions, statutory interpretation is the work of: trial courts, quasi-judicial agencies, other regulatory government agencies, service agencies, government attorneys, private lawyers, trade association executives, interest groups, and citizens deciding the meaning of statutes in coffee shop conversations. News reporters fit in the list somewhere, as do legal scholars.

§ 43–3. Legislative intent. The basic rule of statutory interpretation is that statutes are to be read to further the intent of the legislature. In the governmental scheme of separation of powers, the legislature has the policy-making prerogative. When a legislature has expressed a public policy, the judiciary is to follow that intent. But legislative intent is a vague term, so formulae, canons of construction, practical guides, and folklore have grown up around it.

One problem of intent is that some statutes are very old. The intent of a 19th century legislature may be difficult to translate into today's world. Where should the intent be found? Certainly not in a literal application of the old words to the present day. One suggestion is that the old legislature, with its initial intention, be metaphysically transfered into today's world and its old words be creatively read to produce the kind of justice originally sought. Another route to the same result is to seek an outcome the legislature would desire were it passing the act on the day the statute is being interpreted. It is unwise to interpret a statute in the context of its passage, rather than for the new and changed world. If that were done, each legislature would be forced to repair constantly the work of the past; none of the essential updating of the law could be left to the judiciary and others. There is an economical use of resources if statutes, as well as constitutions, are treated as living documents.

The great theoretical question in statutory interpretation is whether legislative intent is to be discovered through the purpose approach or the plain-meaning approach.

§ 43–4. Purpose approach.

The purpose approach is thought of as the more modern of the two approaches to interpretation, although its roots extend to Heydon's Case (76 E.R. 637, (1584)). Heydon's Case directed courts to ask what was the law before the act, what was the mischief or defect to be corrected, what was the remedy designed to cure the defect and what was the true reason of the remedy? "And then the office of all the judges is always to make such construction as shall suppress the mischief, and advance the remedy and to suppress subtle inventions and invasions for continuance of the mischief . . . and to add force in life to the cure and remedy according to the true intent of the makers of the act, *pro bono publico*." In short, the purpose approach calls for reading a statute to accomplish the objectives of the legislature. To state the proposition is to reveal some circuity underlying the rule, for how is the objective of the legislature determined?

[244]

§ 43–5. Plain-meaning approach and golden rule exception. The plain-meaning approach, usually considered contradictory to the purpose approach, looks at the words enacted by the legislature and gives them their natural and normal meaning. The battles of the legislature concern what the words of the statute shall be. Since the job of the legislature is to enact words, courts cannot ignore the words chosen. The plain-meaning rule recognizes that certain sets of words are sanctified with the policy-making authority of the legislature.

It would be impossible to dissent from the plain-meaning approach if everyone read any set of words to mean exactly the same thing, if draftsmen worked flawlessly, if legislators knew precisely what they intended to say, and if humans could imagine all the future cases which might arise under any legislative enactment. But humans fail at each of these tasks. To deal with reality, courts have engrafted the golden rule exception to the plain-meaning approach. This exception provides that the literal meaning is followed only until it leads "to any absurdity or manifest injustice." Thus courts and all others engaged in statutory interpretation follow the words until the words lead to unjust results, then depart from the literal meaning of the words to the extent necessary to yield just and sensible results.

§ 43–6. A legislature's attitude. Minnesota's statutory construction act reflects typical legislative feeling about how the verbal handiwork of a legislature ought to be read. It includes these two sections (adopted in 1941 and unchanged since then):

645.16 LEGISLATIVE INTENT CONTROLS. The object of all interpretation and construction of laws is to ascertain and effectuate the intention of the legislature. Every law shall be construed, if possible, to give effect to all its provisions.

When the words of a law in their application to an existing situation are clear and free from all ambiguity, the letter of the law shall not be disregarded under the pretext of pursuing the spirit.

When the words of a law are not explicit, the intention of the legislature may be ascertained by considering, among other matters:

> (1) The occasion and necessity for the law;
>
> (2) The circumstances under which it was enacted;
>
> (3) The mischief to be remedied;
>
> (4) The object to be attained;
>
> (5) The former law, if any, including other laws upon the same or similar subjects;

(6) The consequences of a particular interpretation;

(7) The contemporaneous legislative history; and

(8) Legislative and administrative interpretations of the statute.

645.17 PRESUMPTIONS IN ASCERTAINING LEGISLATIVE INTENT. In ascertaining the intention of the legislature the courts may be guided by the following presumptions:

(1) The legislature does not intend a result that is absurd, impossible of execution, or unreasonable;

(2) The legislature intends the entire statute to be effective and certain;

(3) The legislature does not intend to violate the constitution of the United States or of this state;

(4) When a court of last resort has construed the language of a law, the legislature in subsequent laws on the same subject matter intends the same construction to be placed upon such language, and

(5) The legislature intends to favor the public interest as against any private interest.

What has this legislature been saying through the years? First: pay attention to the words we write (the plain-meaning approach); but don't make us look ridiculous by giving absurd meanings to our enactments (the golden rule exception); and furthermore: what we really want is to achieve our policy objectives (the purpose approach). A cynic might conclude a legislature enacting these or similar provisions is sending conflicting messages. A more accurate view is that the legislature, seeing merit in all the rules, invites courts to pursue with wisdom and understanding the task of statutory interpretation, using each of the approaches as appropriate.

§ 43–7. Opponents' contribution to intent. Supporters of bills do not manufacture legislative intent without help from the opposition; the contributions from opponents may be undesired, but they are legally relevant. A controversial bill usually makes its way through a legislative institution only after significant compromises are inserted to accommodate opponents and lukewarm supporters. Discussion of legislative intent often assumes a legislature passes bills without dissent, in perfect harmony. In reality, the legislature fights vigorously over changes in sections, phrases, and words. Changes may be bitterly opposed by sponsors but nonetheless be approved by a majority of the body. When a court, agency, or lawyer interprets an act, the limitations are just as much a part of the legislative intent as is the primary goal of the sponsors. Because the significant words of limitation may not be reflected in legislative reports, speeches, or official explanations, these materials deserve limited attention as a guide to legislative intent, especially when set against the actual words of the statute.

B. PARTNERSHIP OF COURT AND LEGISLATURE

§ 44–1. Advantage of shared responsibility. The statutory provisions cited in § 43–6 suggest a legislative desire for lawmaking help from courts as they interpret statutes. Such a partnership makes sense, for the separate lawmaking institutions of society have differing strengths and weaknesses. The strength of the legislature is in its power to set the law in new directions, to establish comprehensive programs attacking the problems of society, to generalize rules which can be made accessible and understandable to most of the community. The weakness of the legislature is an inability to imagine the infinite variety of circumstances in which its rules will be applied and to draft the limitations and exceptions required to fit all these circumstances. The adjudicatory process is strong at the precise point the legislative institution is weak. The judiciary

deals with specific fact situations.   Courts examine the actions of the parties and with perfect
hindsight find just resolutions of disputes.   Decisions in appellate court cases produce narrow
rules, but they are rules of precision and justice.

This   perspective   on   the   complementary
strengths of our lawmaking institutions supports
the pragmatic combination of the plain-meaning
approach, the golden rule exception, and the purpose approach followed by wise judges.   The combination capitalizes on the power of the judiciary
to establish refined and detailed precedents (legal
rules) for future cases.   It also capitalizes on the
strength of the legislature for generalization, leaving to the courts the tasks of smoothing rough
edges, mitigating harsh results, adding overlooked   distinctions,   and   repairing   imperfect
draftsmanship.

§ 44–2. **Historical conflicts.**   The historical
relationships between courts and legislatures are
perceived with the same distortions that plague
legislatures in daily press reports of their activity.   Conflict gets the attention.   Cooperation and
accommodation—and partnership—do not make
news.   As a result journalists, historians, and legal commentators, tempted to tell more interesting tales, convey the inaccurate impression that
courts are antagonistic to legislatures.   The con-
clusion follows that courts are not likely to help

legislatures. This view started when the English parliament first struggled to win power for itself and challenged the power of the monarch. Kings fought to retain power and to construct what checks they could around the legislative branch. Allied with the crown were his appointed judges. Judges used every bit of ambiguity in parliamentary acts to preserve lawmaking and governing authority for themselves and for the monarch who appointed them. History reports those occasions when judges frustrated the legislature; but the occasions when judicial decisions advanced legislative objectives without conflict are lost in the routine of the law.

In this century the dramatic conflict arising from judicial use of the doctrine of economic due process to strike down state and federal regulatory legislation, President Roosevelt's court-packing plan, and several decades of powerful opinions on judicial restraint by Justice Frankfurter taught generations of law students and scholars that legislature and court are instinctive rivals, if not enemies. Lost from view were the hundreds of legislative mistakes overlooked and corrected by judges sympathetic with legislative goals or, more to the point, respectful of the legislative prerogatives in policy making.

§ 44–3. Merger of constituencies. Study of judicial and legislative relations must take account of their respective constituencies. When legislative power first developed, parliament and monarch came to office through different conduits—one by election, the other by inheritance. Conflict was normal, inevitable. Different forces in the society were allied with each. The more recent major conflict of court and legislature also had roots in divergent constituencies. In the early 20th century the life-tenured federal judges had received their appointments from the politicians of the pre-progressive era. Those politicans had picked judges from corporate, especially railroad, law practices. Legislatures, on the other hand, were shaped by a political tide of reform and populism. Both court and legislature were part of the democratic political system, but new attitudes came to the two branches at different times. Unfortunately, the judges holding over from the prior period in that one era had a peculiarly perverse antagonism to the new age. The situation is not likely to recur.

A more accurate expectation for the future is that judges and legislators will generally march to the same drummer, although dislocation may arise occasionally from a time lag affecting one branch or the other. The courts, because they listen to persuasive attorneys argue for justice based on specific facts, may be ahead of legislatures; or, isolated from political pressure, they may temporarily fall behind the electorate and the legislative branch. Such temporary conflicts are bearable when the legal system takes advantage of the best characteristics of both branches. There is more to be gained than lost if courts free themselves from the literal words of a statute, when to do so is appropriate. Common sense and justice often require this if law is to serve the best interests of citizens who are the constituents of both judge and legislator. The need for courts to respect the importance of the words of a statute, but not to exaggerate their reliability, is obvious to those who understand legislative procedures, the forces at work on the legislature, the burdens of legislative work, and the low legislative priority given to law reform and to making private law rules.

Courts also have the responsibility to insure that the basic provisions of the constitution remain intact; their isolation from political pressure helps them carry out this role because they are free to take the long perspective and need not be swayed by overwhelming political pressure.

§ 44–4. Reasoning from the statute. Dean Roscoe Pound in 1908 persuasively urged courts to borrow from the civil law system the practice of using legislative acts as guides to just decisions. Legal scholars continue to urge that statutes not be ignored in the development of the common law. This idea encompasses more than

use of the purpose approach to statutory interpretation. It suggests that courts might give
statutes the same intellectual respect they accord
judicial precedents. If a case falls within the logic of a judicial precedent, but outside its holding,
a court reasons by analogy and applies the logic
of the precedent to the new fact situation. Similarly, if a case falls within the logic, justice, and
policy of a statute, but outside the legislature's
actual or conscious intent, a court can reason
from the statute by analogy to find a just rule for
the new fact situation. The court need not,
because the legislature did not cover the case in
the statute, presume a legislative intention to
have the case decided by an old rule which does
not fit it as well as a rule consistent with the
statute.

§ 44–5. **Aids to interpretation; legislative history.** Statutory interpretation does not end with
the words of the statute or with the facts of the
case to which the statute may apply. Extrinsic
materials can be used, including knowledge about
the circumstances surrounding passage of the legislation. Problems which pushed the legislature
to action are particularly relevant; the context of
passage is pertinent to the intent. General
knowledge may provide the background necessary
to interpret a legislative act; sometimes there is
a desire for more precise information.

STATUTORY INTERPRETATION   Ch. 13

The natural place to look is in the legislative records concerning the act. But action which is natural is not always wise. Legislative history can raise more questions than it answers. One legislator cannot speak for the full institution. Therefore remarks in debate and in committee reports are unreliable guides to intent; they are also inconsistent. Legislators who win battles to insert words into statutes do not amend speeches. One who interprets the act by its proponents' speeches, rather than by the legislature's amendatory words, is relying on weak authority.

Another defect in use of legislative history is the great cost involved. The words of an act are readily available. They are short and authoritative. Legislative debates, studies, committee reports, and official records are difficult to find, lengthy, self-contradictory, and of uncertain reliability. The legislature is as faithfully served by looking at its enacted words as by relying on dubious speeches and reports. To determine the meaning of an act using its words is more economical than using its history. The more expensive technique favors wealthy interests over those with limited resources.

Congress produces significant amounts of official history. Use of this history is well established in practice, although the same problems apply. State legislatures produce less complete history and its use in interpreting state statutes is spotty. Courts in the future ought to discourage the use of legislative history, and to rely instead on respectful and creative reading of the legislative acts themselves.

C. CANONS OF STATUTORY CONSTRUCTION

§ 45–1. More for writers than readers. The rules of construction, although formulated in the context of statutory interpretation, are more valuable to the writers of bills than to the readers of acts. For the writer of statutes, the canons provide discipline and a firm logical base for his work. If the writer uses the logic of the canons, he makes future interpretation of his words easier. If the writer forgets the canons and the reader remembers them, trouble is certain. For these reasons, canons are more important to draftsmen than to interpreters.

The reader must be flexible, practical, tolerant, helpful, and realistic about the imperfections of legislative work. Neat rules will never fit the interpretation part of legislation for those rules are overlooked at the bill-writing stage. Legislative purpose and the need for justice in the case at hand are better guides to how a statute should be read than all the canons of construction multiplied ten times. Canons are, however, valid signposts which help the reader correctly interpret statutory words. They are worth attention from more than just those who work in legislative institutions.

§ 45–2. Strict or liberal interpretation.

A boilerplate provision in many acts is the instruction that the act be given a liberal construction to implement its objectives. The provision appears often in general statutory construction acts, which means it is directed at every act passed by a legislature. When used in single acts, the clause encourages the purpose approach in interpretation of that particular act. When used in the general statutory construction act, the clause may change slightly the basic approach to statutory interpretation in that jurisdiction.

With or without the boilerplate provision, two kinds of statutes are given strict construction; these are penal and tax statutes. Strict interpretation means that ambiguities are decided against the state, not that the words are read literally. The principle of strict construction is related to the rule of contract law which holds that ambiguities in contracts are resolved against the party who wrote the contract. The state writes penal and tax laws, so it loses on all ambiguities. Strict and literal are not synonymous in statutory construction, although confusion of the terms is common. Literal goes with the plain-meaning rule; strict goes with the question of who gets the benefit of any doubt. Strict interpretation means that to collect a tax or to impose a criminal penalty the state must make the statute unambiguous.

§ 45–3. Intent to change law; whole statute given effect. It is presumed under the canons of interpretation that a legislature does not go through the work of passing an act without intending to change the law. Courts reading statutes struggle to find in each act modification of prior law, even if by its terms the act seems to do nothing. This canon of construction forces participants in the legislative process to resist the apparently meaningless bill. Courts will try to insert some meaning into every bill passed by a legislature, so empty bills are dangerous. Coupled with the rule that an intent to change the law is presumed is a corollary rule that courts are to give meaning to each provision of the act. Therefore, meaningless sections are also dangerous. The two rules show more distrust of courts than other rules of construction; the rules imply that courts would like to give effect only to those provisions or acts which they approve.

To apply these rules, when provisions or acts appear inconsistent, one act or section is read, if at all possible, as an exception to the other more general provision or act. A special act prevails over a more general act; a specific provision prevails over a general provision. When acts are so inconsistent that both cannot be given effect, the later act prevails over the earlier act, since it is the more recent expression of legislative will.

The presumption of intent to change the law does not apply to law revisions. When the legislature enacts a revision to clean up the form of the law, rather than to improve its substance, the presumption is just the opposite of the usual rule. Then new words are read to carry forward the old meaning, even if through faulty draftsmanship they say something different.

§ 45–4. **Repeal; non-use.** The canon of construction that instructs readers to give meaning to the whole act is consistent with the presumption or canon of construction that repeal is not implied. If the legislature wants to eliminate a section of law, it ought to repeal that provision explicitly; until it does so, effort is made to give meaning to the retained provision, even in the face of contradictory later acts. Other canons relevant to repeal are: the repeal of an act which repealed another act does not revive the previously repealed act; a statute is not repealed because there is no reason for it to be continued in the law; and a statute is not repealed automatically because it is not used.

§ 45–5. **Some bits of Latin.** Several canons of construction based on obvious logic are expressed in Latin phrases, perhaps to conceal their simplicity. The Latin phrases make those who use them appear scholarly; the English translations make the user sound sensible and clearheaded; using both may be best. All are qualified by the basic rule that legislative intent controls.

(a) *Noscitur a sociis* (known by its associates) —When a word has different meanings at different times, its meaning in a statute may be determined from the words it is associated with. *Doctor,* for example, used with one set of words means medical doctor; in another set of words it includes chiropractors, podiatrists and optometrists; in a further set of words, it includes doctors of philosophy and even possessors of juris doctor degrees.

(b) *Ejusdem generis* (of the same class)— When a general word or phrase is used in a list, its general meaning is limited to things which fit with the more specific items in the list. This rule is usually applied when a list ends with a phrase like "and other written documents." The rule adds by implication the phrase "of the same type as those which are in this list."

(c) *Expressio unius est exclusio alterious* (expression of one excludes others)—This is a rule of negative implication or backspin. If the drafter of a statute mentions one circumstance specif-

STATUTORY INTERPRETATION   Ch. 13

ically, the implication is that other circumstances which just as logically could have been mentioned were intentionally omitted. This rule is a particular problem in legislation when a lobbyist refuses to be satisfied with a general limitation and insists on a specific exclusionary clause to "take care of my client." If he gets his clause inserted, the general limitation may be undermined and the whole statute thrown out of balance.

(d) *Pari materia* (of the same matter)—When more than one statute relates to a subject, each must be considered when any one is being read. The reason for this is that the whole body of law must be kept consistent with itself; one act must not be read to negate another act. Also a word should carry its meaning from one statute over into another related statute, just as a word should carry one meaning throughout a single enactment. If a different meaning is intended, a different word should be used.

§ 45–6.   Some bits of English. Several canons of construction have escaped translation into Latin.

(a) Words and phrases are construed according to ordinary rules of grammar and ordinary dictionary meanings.

(b) Technical and legal words and words with special meanings are construed according to the technical, legal, or special meaning appropriate to the context of the statute.

(c) Words of any gender, number, or tense may be read to include any other gender, number, or tense appropriate to the context. Generally statutes are written in the masculine gender, the singular number and the present tense.

(d) Interpretations of statutes contemporaneous with their passage are relevant guides to later interpretation.

(e) Interpretations of similar statutes in other jurisdictions are relevant guides to interpretation of statutes.

INDEX

INDEX
References are to Pages

INDEX

INDEX

INDEX

INDEX

INDEX

INDEX

INDEX

INDEX

INDEX